Expansion, Trade and Industry

1750 - 1900

J F AYLETT

Hodder & Stoughton
LONDON SYDNEY AUCKLAND

ACKNOWLEDGEMENTS

The Publishers would like to thank the following for permission to reproduce illustrations in this volume:
Guildhall Library, Corporation of London/ The Bridgeman Art Library -cover. Mary Evans Picture Library p4; p7 lower; p9; p18 right; p19 top left; p24; p46. Mary Evans Picture Library/Bruce Castle Museum p29. Bedfordshire Record Office p5 top right. The Tate Gallery, London p6 right; p44 left; p64 right. Nordiska Museet, Stockholm p7 top. National Museums of Scotland p8 left. The Mansell Collection p8 right; p10 left; p13 both; p14; p24 lower left; p20 top right; p23 left; p28 right; p45; p51 left; p52; p53 both; p55 lower left. Lancashire County Council, Helmshore Textile Museum p10 right. Manchester Public Libraries p12; p38. Ironbridge Gorge Museum Trust p15. The Hulton-Deutsch Picture Company p16; p48 left; p50; p64 left. Department of Prints & Drawings, The British Museum, London p17; p28 left; p60 right; p69 top. Yorkshire Mining Museum p18 top left. Reproduced by permission of The Science Museum, London p20 top left; p27 lower left; p32 left; p33. Cyfartha Castle Museum & Art Gallery p20 lower. David Grant p23 right. Merthyr Tydfil Central Library Records p25. National Trust Photographic Library/David Cripps p26 left. Royal Holloway & Bedford New College/ The Bridgeman Art Library p26 right. c. Lord Romsey, Broadlands p27 top. British Waterways Archive p31 right. Southampton Art Gallery p32 right. Reproduced by permission of the Birmingham Museum & Art Gallery p34 left. Great Western Railway Museum/Thamesdown Borough Council p34 right. By permission of the Keeper of the National Railway Museum, York p35 both. Thames Television International Ltd p37 both. The British Library, London/The Bridgeman Art Library p39. The National Portrait Gallery, London p41. The Communist Party Library & Archives p42. Windsor Castle Royal Archives c. 1993 Her Majesty the Queen p43 top. The Illustrated London News Picture Library p43 lower. Royal Academy of Arts, London p44 right. Public Record Office c. Crown Copyright p47 left. The Board of Trustees of the National Museums & Galleries on Merseyside, Walker Art Gallery p47 right. The National Gallery of Canada, Ottawa p48 right. Lester Smith p51 right; p73 left; p73 top right; p73 lower right; p76 right. Wilberforce House, Hull City Museums & Art Galleries p54 left. The Bettman Archive p54 right. New York Public Library p55 top. Liverpool Libraries & Record Office p57 both. Doug Lear p58 left; p59 both; p72 top left; p72 right; p79 left. Rex Nan Kivell Collection, National Library of Australia p58 right. British Library Reproductions p60 top left. Sainsbury Archive p60 lower left. Wales Tourist Board p61. University College, Dublin p63 left. By permission of the Board of Trustees of The National Library of Ireland p63 right; p65 right. Johannesburg Art Gallery p65 left. Centre for Oxfordshire Studies p66 top right. Reproduced by permission of the Board of Trustees, The Victoria and Albert Museum, London p67 top; p79 right. The Royal Collection c. 1993 Her Majesty the Queen p67 lower. Paisley Museum & Art Galleries, Renfrew District Council p68 right. Trade Union Congress Picture Library p70 left. The John Gorman Collection p70 right; p71. Harrogate Museums & Art Galleries/ The Bridgeman Art Library p74 left. Mander & Mitcheson Theatre Collection p74 right. Greater London Authority Picture Library p75 left. BBC Photograph Library p75 right. Tate Gallery/ The Bridgeman Art Library p76 left. Mike Williams Photography p77 right. Billy Kay p78 left.

The Publishers would also like to thank the following for permission to reproduce copyright material:
Extract reproduced from The *Day The Universe Changed* by James Burke with the permission of BBC Enterprises Limited; Frank Cass Publishers for the extract from *Victorian Working Women*; George Philip for the extract from *The World Changes*; John Murray (Publishers) Ltd for the extract from *Years of Change* by John Patrick and Mollie Packham; Oxford University Press for the extract from *Early Victorian England*, edited by GM Young (1934); Thomas Nelson and Sons Ltd for the extracts from *House of History* by Dorothy Gordon; Routledge for the extracts from *The Industrial and Commercial Revolutions* by L Knowles and *By the Sweat of their Brow* by Angela V John; Virago Press for the extract from *Bombers and Mash* by R Minns.
Every effort has been made to trace and acknowledge ownership of copyright. The Publishers will be glad to make suitable arrangements with any copyright holder whom it has not been possible to contact.

Illustrations by Philip Page

British Library Cataloguing in Publication Data

Aylett, J. F.
Expansion, Trade and Industry,
1750-1900. – (Past Historic Series)
I. Title II. Series
941.07

ISBN 0 340 54827 4

First published 1993
Impression number 10 9 8 7 6 5 4 3 2 1
Year 1998 1997 1996 1995 1994 1993

Typeset by Litho Link Limited, Welshpool, Powys, Wales.
Printed in Great Britain for the educational publishing division of Hodder & Stoughton Ltd, Mill Road, Dunton Green. Sevenoaks, Kent by Scotprint Ltd, Musselburgh, Scotland

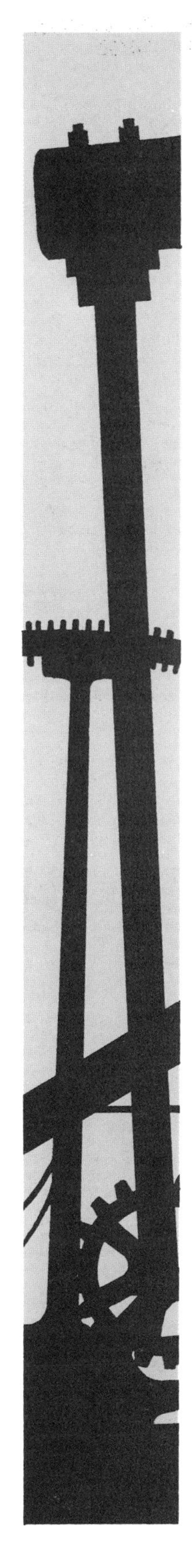

CONTENTS

In the middle of the 19th century, a German boy called Otto Lilienthal used to strap linen wings to his arms and run down hillsides. He wanted to fly. As you know, he wasn't the first. But he studied it more seriously than most. He even wrote a book about his studies of how birds flew.

By 1894, he was launching himself from hillsides, using a glider. On one occasion, he glided over 220 metres at up to 30mph. Two years later, trying out a new device to operate the rudder, he lost control and crashed. His back was broken and he died in hospital the next day.

But many people had read his descriptions of the pleasures of gliding. They included two Americans, Wilbur and Orville Wright, who were determined to continue his work. We know this because they wrote about it. It is through sources such as these that historians study the past.

Highlighted words are explained in the glossary on page 80.

1 A FARMING REVOLUTION

A The village green, shown in a late 18th-century painting.

In 1750, much of England's food was still being grown in strips in big open fields. Many villages had three or four of these and nearly all the villagers shared the strips. Around the village was common land, where they grazed their animals.

It was not the most efficient way of producing food. People could waste hours walking from one strip to another; weeds spread easily; in some villages, one complete field was left fallow every year to get back its goodness. Yet, in most years, the system provided the villagers with all the food they needed for themselves. Few farmers set out to produce extra food to sell.

But the population was growing fast in the 18th century. The new towns which were growing up could not provide all their own food: they relied on the villages. Town dwellers needed bread; the farmers needed to grow more corn.

As long as everyone shared the strips, this was not possible. You could not experiment, unless everyone agreed. Nor could you breed better animals. On the common grazing land, diseases spread fast.

The better-off landowners wanted to enclose the open fields and the common land. In other words, they wanted to create separate farms; each field would have a hedge or fence around it.

If everyone agreed, they went ahead and enclosed the land. But poorer villagers often objected. When that happened, the landowners had to ask Parliament's permission. Parliament usually agreed.

Commissioners then turned up in the village and started to share out the land. Anyone who owned some was guaranteed a share. But it was not cheap enclosing land. It cost money to get Parliament to pass an Act allowing the enclosure to happen. There were hedges, fences and new roads to pay for – and the commissioners' fees. (Their expenses alone could cost £3 a day.)

The poor often could not afford it. In any case, the common land was usually enclosed, too. Unless you owned a field, there was nowhere to graze your animals.

Many villagers simply couldn't prove the land was theirs. Perhaps they had lost the piece of paper to prove it. Or perhaps they had just built their house on common land. Either way, they received nothing after enclosure. So, many of them sold their land and became labourers, working for someone else. Others went to find work in a town.

It was a huge upheaval for the villagers. Historians call the changes *the agricultural revolution*. Enclosure was just one part of it.

Was enclosure a sudden change?

B *The World Changes* (a school textbook, 1954).
Each year one-third of all the ploughland of the village had to lie fallow with only sheep and cows grazing over it. Yet what else could be done? The farmers of Britain knew no better way to keep the soil healthy until the eighteenth century. [Then] some of them visited Holland and learned new ideas from the Dutch.

C C J Hall: *A Short History of English Agriculture* (1924).
In 1750 a great part of England still [had] open fields. [There had been a] very slow movement towards enclosure [since the 16th century]. A few counties, such as Suffolk, Essex, and Kent [were] almost entirely enclosed. Others, such as Norfolk and Northamptonshire, were partly enclosed; but in many others enclosures were almost unknown.

D David Evans: *Wales in Modern Times* (1979).
In Wales, the [open] field system had never really existed. Enclosures were mainly [made of] the common fields and hillsides. It was there that the small farmers found pasture for their animals. In addition, they could claim wood and turf.

Secondary sources may disagree for all sorts of reasons. For instance, circumstances vary from one area to another. Changes often do not affect everyone in the same way.

E Surveyors measuring out village land in about 1798.

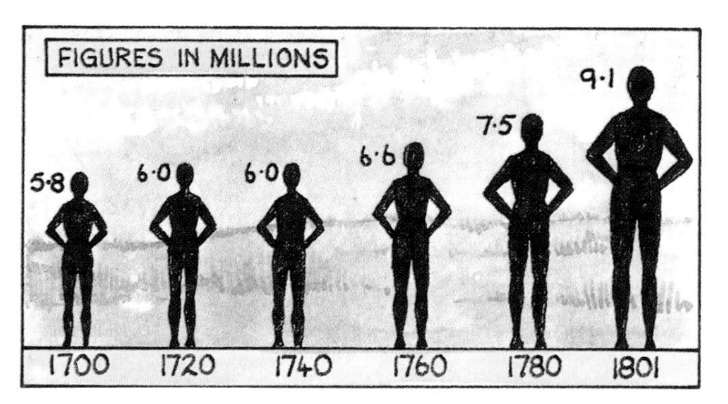

F An estimate of the population of England and Wales in millions. (The first accurate figures were provided by the first census in 1801.)

1 a) Look at source A. How were these things useful to villagers: (i) the grass; (ii) the trees?
b) What sort of work is the woman doing on the green?
c) How would this help her family?
d) What evidence is there that the pace of country life was slow?

2 a) Why was more food needed in the 18th century?
b) Why did better-off farmers want to enclose land? (Give at least two reasons.)
c) Why might poorer farmers object?

3 a) Look at source F. During which period did the population grow fastest?
b) How do these figures help to explain the agricultural revolution?

4 a) How do sources B and C disagree? Give a detailed answer.
b) How does source D add to your understanding of enclosure?
c) Do you think the agricultural revolution happened suddenly? Explain your answer.

IMPROVING FARMING

The richer landowners did well out of enclosures. They could now experiment on the enclosed fields of their new farms. As a result, they grew more food and made bigger profits.

The changes they made did not happen overnight. In fact, one of the most important changes happened gradually over 200 years or more. This was the end of the system of leaving one field fallow each year to get back its goodness.

In the 17th century, Sir Richard Weston started sowing crops like turnips or clover, instead of leaving one fallow field. Over four years, each field would grow a different crop each year. The system became known as the Norfolk Rotation. It had great advantages, as this diagram shows.

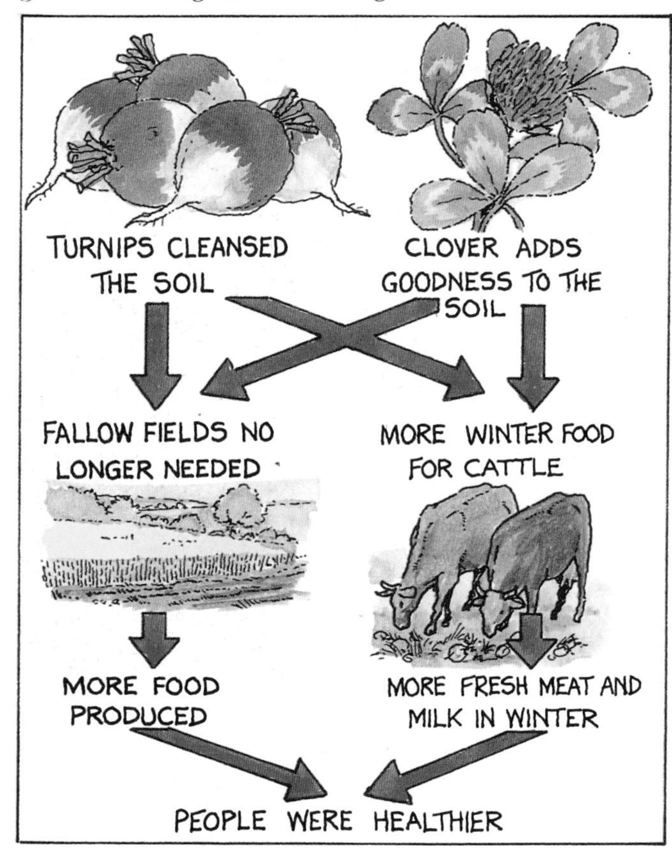

This new system did not catch on everywhere at once. In fact, it did not become popular until the 18th century when Lord Townshend made changes on his Norfolk farm. One of these changes was growing turnips. Townshend was famous enough to make other farmers look carefully at what he was doing. People were soon calling him 'Turnip' Townshend.

A Berkshire farmer called Jethro Tull was another man whose idea did not catch on suddenly. He had invented a seed drill which sowed seeds in straight lines. It saved seed and it produced bigger crops.

Tull wrote about it in a book in 1731 but it was another century before his machine became popular. This was partly because the early machines had problems; it was also because some of Tull's other ideas did not work, so some farmers were suspicious of his drill.

Other farmers turned their attention to animals. The sheep and cattle which grazed on the common land had been skinny creatures. They mated at random and it was impossible to control disease.

Robert Bakewell, who farmed in Leicestershire, set about changing all that. With the population rising, there was a demand for good mutton – and plenty of it. Bakewell carefully chose sheep for breeding to produce fatter animals.

Bakewell's New Leicester breed quickly spread. This painting shows his rams being hired out to other farmers. During the century, the weight of his sheep doubled. Much of this was fat – but at least you could eat it.

Bakewell also experimented with cattle. His Longhorn cattle were almost as famous as his sheep. But even better-known were the Durham Shorthorns, bred by the Colling Brothers in Durham. Once again, these improvements did not spread overnight.

Meanwhile, a Yorkshire weaver was busy looking after his pig. This was no ordinary pig. Joseph Tuley and his wife would even wash it and take it for walks. When money was short, the couple went without food themselves – just so long as their pig did not go hungry. We should be grateful. From his pig was developed the Large White pig which is still common in Britain today.

B Farm workers threshing grain in 1888. The fiddler's tune kept them in time.

C The threshing machine was invented in 1785 but did not become common until the 1820s.

The changes in farming did not happen everywhere at the same time. There were many reasons for this. One was that farmers could choose whether to use a new idea or not. Some chose not to do so. Try to think of other reasons.

1. What changes were introduced by these farmers: (a) Sir Richard Weston, (b) Jethro Tull, (c) Robert Bakewell and (d) the Colling brothers?
2. a) Give at least two examples from the text of changes which spread slowly.
   b) Give an example from the sources of another change which spread slowly.
   c) Why did change come slowly? (Use *both* pages.)
3. This question is about consequences.
   a) What were the results of growing turnips and clover?
   b) How did farmers benefit from all these changes?
   c) How did other people benefit?
   d) What do you think was the most important result of these changes? Give reasons.
   e) Think of sources B and C. Would there have been any disadvantages? Explain your answer.

2 TOWARDS AN INDUSTRIAL REVOLUTION

A A painting of a home in Perthshire, Scotland.

The biggest industry after farming was the cloth industry. After all, everyone needs clothes. In fact, cloth was being made just about everywhere in Britain. Most of it was made by hand and people made it *at home*. So this system of production is called *the Domestic System*.

Much of this work was done part-time by people whose main income came from farming. There was work for the whole family. Indeed, one family could do the whole process of turning the wool into cloth. Most of the equipment was small; the biggest item was a loom and even that could be fitted into the living-room.

However, five or six spinners were needed to keep one weaver supplied with enough wool. So it had become common for the different parts of the process to be done in different places. Sometimes, yarn was carried hundreds of miles before it reached the weaver.

Someone had to organise all this. It was often someone with capital – in other words, money. Usually, it was a rich merchant, known as a clothier. He needed to be well-off because it could take many months before the wool had been turned into cloth to sell.

First, the raw wool was taken to people who would card and spin it. The spun yarn was then taken to the weaver. Finally, the woven cloth was collected and the next batch of yarn delivered. The richest clothiers did not do any of this themselves: they paid agents to do the fetching and carrying.

The clothier paid piece rates – so much money for each item made. He could almost force his workers to take whatever pay he offered. The workers were at a disadvantage: they needed the income. Women and children were often exploited.

The cloth was produced in much the same way it had been for centuries. People provided the muscle power which did most of the work. But, in 1750, the population was increasing. More people needed more clothes. The domestic workers couldn't keep up – and change was just around the corner.

"A Cobler there was & he lived in a Stall
Which served him for Parlour & Kitchen & hall" !–

B In 1750, the domestic system was used for making most goods. The family in this cartoon made shoes (1828).

> Different sources may give different views of the past. Writers were quick to compare the domestic system with the factories which came later. Many writers made clear their point of view in what they wrote.

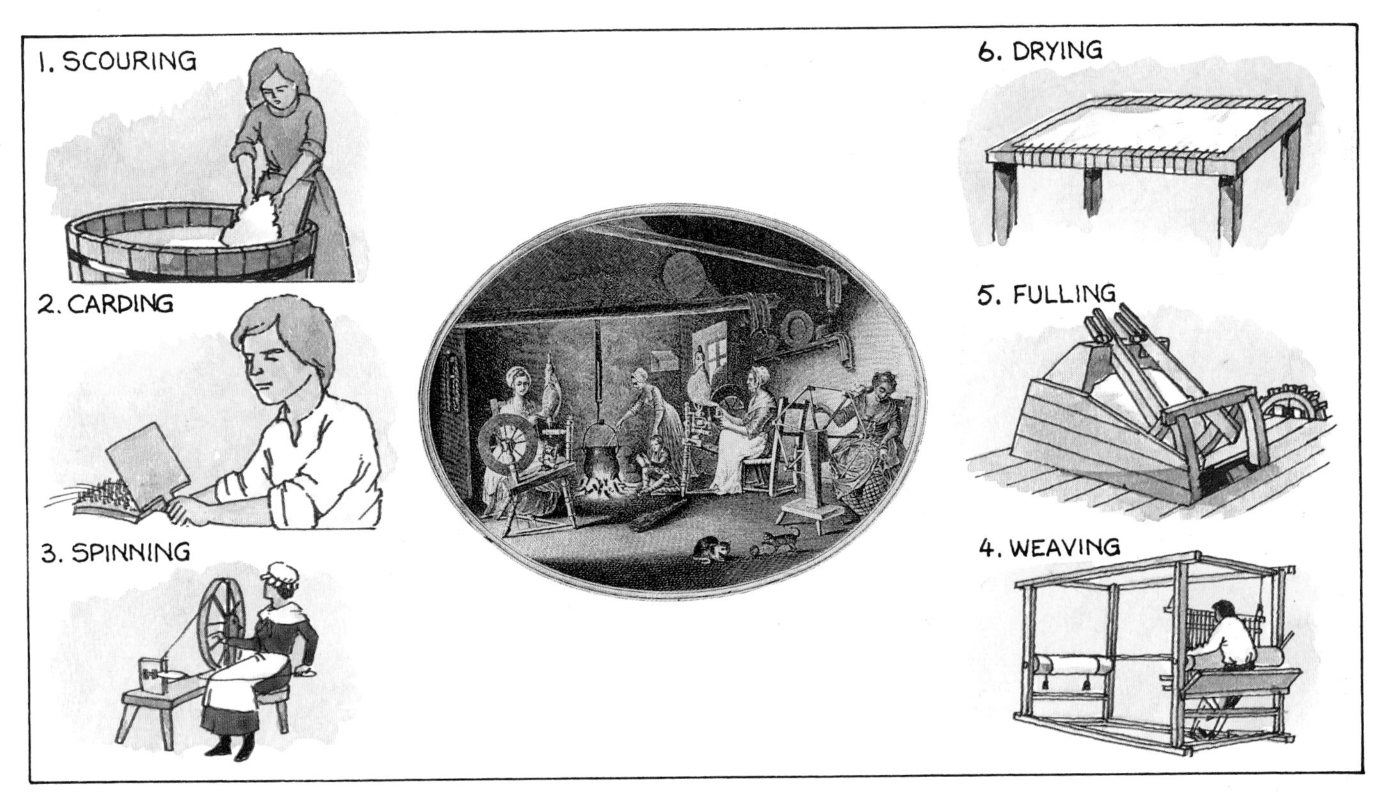

What were working conditions like?

C Dr Andrew Ure: *The Cotton Manufacture of Great Britain* (1836).

The workshop of the weaver was a rural cottage; when he was tired of work he could go into his little garden, and tend it with the spade or hoe.

D Friedrich Engels: *The Working Class* (1844).

Their children grew up in the fresh country air. If they could help their parents at work, it was only occasionally. Of eight or twelve hours' work for them there was no question.

E A modern historian, Wanda Neff, wrote this in *Victorian Working Women* (1929).

Even spinning before the cottage doorway in the sunshine [had] its hardships. Two shillings and sixpence (12.5p) was the average weekly earning of the woman spinner. Poverty and the need of the weaver for [yarn] compelled [her to work] long hours. The weavers commonly worked 14, 15 and 16 hours a day.

F W Cooke Taylor: *Notes on a Tour of the Manufacturing Districts of Lancashire* (1842).

These were really the days of infant slavery. The creatures were set to work as soon as they could crawl and their parents were the hardest of task-masters.

G The stages in the production of woollen cloth. The centre picture shows Protestant linen workers in Ireland (late 18th century).

1 Explain the meaning of each of these words: loom; yarn; capital; clothier; piece rate.

2 a) Look at sources A, B and G. Were these people well-off or not? In each case, explain how you decided.
b) For each source, give a mark out of ten to show how realistic you think it is. (Think of your last answer.)
c) Look again at the picture to which you gave fewest marks. Explain why you think it is least reliable.

3 a) Read sources C to F. Which writers give the view that life as a domestic worker was pleasant?
b) How do sources D and E disagree?
c) Write a paragraph describing the domestic system, using only sources C and D.
d) Now, write a paragraph describing the system, using only sources E and F.
e) What does this teach you about the use of historical sources?

WHY DID FACTORIES DEVELOP?

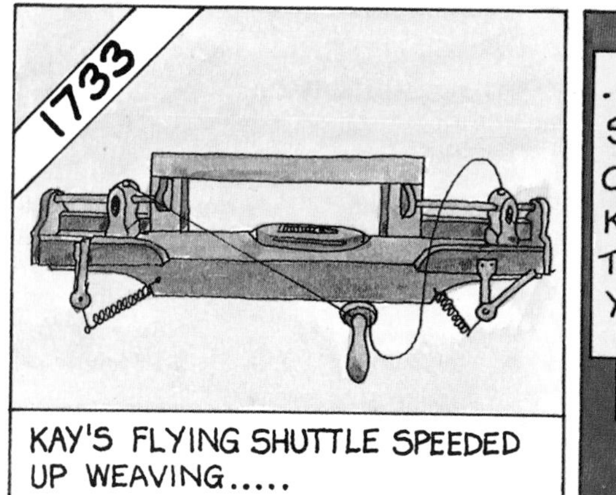

Two early inventions in the cotton industry. Each inventor had his house attacked as a result of his invention.

When change did come, it came first in the cotton industry. Cotton cloth had become popular. Merchants could make good profits from selling cotton cloth and they wanted more of it produced. So people looked for ways to make the production process quicker.

The two inventions shown above helped: Kay's flying shuttle speeded up the weaving; Hargreaves' spinning jenny speeded up the spinning. Each could be used by people working at home. Even the new spinning jenny was simple, small and easily made. You could buy one for about £2.50.

While the domestic system was still used for cotton manufacture, silk was already being made in factories. By 1750, there were a number of silk **mills** in England — but there were no cotton mills. Why, then, in the 1770s, did cotton manufacture begin to shift to factories?

There is no one answer to that question. However, we can be certain who was responsible. His name was Richard Arkwright. You may remember him as the man who started out in life as a barber's apprentice.

In 1769, Arkwright took out a **patent** on a spinning frame. He claimed it could spin stronger yarn than a jenny – and do it more cheaply. He first used his frame in a mill in Nottingham, where it was powered by a horse.

Two years later, he built a mill at Cromford on the River Derwent. This ran on water power. By 1788, there were 143 mills like his, including 19 in Scotland. Instead of working at home, thousands of people worked in large factories instead.

But this still does not answer the question: why did the factory system develop? Historians have given different answers to this question.

A A spinster (spinner) is shown working at home in this 18th century picture.

B This water frame came from Arkwright's mill at Cromford. It has 96 spindles.

C This explanation was given by E Baines in *History of the Cotton Manufacture in Great Britain* (1835).

In 1769 [Arkwright] took out a patent for a machine for twisting yarn by rollers. When he installed it in a new mill at Cromford, which was turned by a water wheel, the machine was called the *water frame*. The machines needed more space than could be found in a cottage and more power than the human arm. They were so heavy they could not be turned by any power then known but that of water.

D R L Hills gave a different explanation in *Cotton Spinning* (1977).

Arkwright could have made more machines and sold them locally or he could have allowed his machines to be built on a small scale and used in cottages. It would have been quite easy for people to have driven these machines themselves and had them at home. But Arkwright's business sense told him that his machine had much greater potential because it could be set up in factories and driven by power.

E Another modern historian, Professor Mantoux, wrote this about Arkwright:

In order to set up large factories, to engage [and train workers], to enforce strict discipline, he needed a [special] energy and activity. These were qualities which most inventors never had. Without [them] their inventions could not have [led to] a new industrial system. It was Arkwright who really created the modern factory.

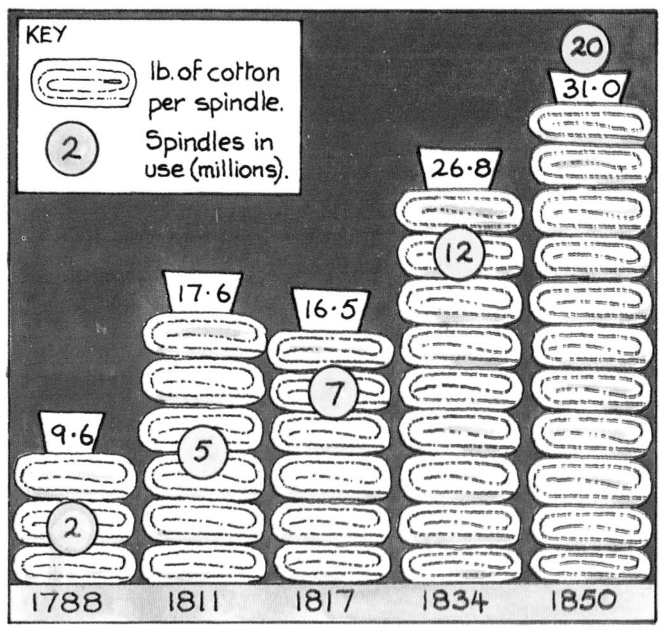

F How cotton production increased from 1788 to 1850. There were millions more spindles, each holding more yarn.

These drawings show some possible causes why Arkwright built factories. Which are the most likely causes?

Events rarely have just one cause or one consequence (result). Often, different *kinds* of causes can bring about an event. An invention can cause change – or a single human being can bring about change. If money is involved, there may be an economic cause, too.

1 a) What caused the invention of (i) the spinning jenny and (ii) the water frame?
b) Write down at least one result of each invention.

2 a) Look at source A. Why can't she compete with the water frame in source B?
b) What may happen to her? (List as many *possible* consequences as you can.)

3 a) Sources C, D and E suggest three different reasons why cotton production moved into factories. What are the three reasons?
b) Suggest at least one reason why the writers disagree.
c) Look at source B. Do you think this was too large to be used at home? Give reasons.
d) In your own words, explain why you think cotton started being spun in factories.
e) What do you think was the main cause? Explain how you decided.

WORK FOR THE CHILDREN

The first mills used water power. So they were often built in lonely valleys, far from towns and cities. This gave the mill-owners a problem. They had to find workers.

However, the machines were very simple to operate. Most of the work could easily be done by women or children – and it usually was. The two main jobs were repairing broken cotton threads (piecing) and cleaning under the machines (scavenging). Children's nimble fingers and small bodies were ideal for these tasks.

Children were easy to come by. Most large towns had a workhouse. The officials in charge were grateful to mill-owners who took pauper children off their hands and made them unpaid apprentices.

However, Arkwright did not employ pauper apprentices at Cromford. He advertised for families to live in the town. He employed some women but, mostly, children. By 1790, Arkwright's spinners earned 16p a week. They worked 13 hours a day, six days a week.

The long hours were not unusual in those days – and most mills were probably better than a life in the workhouse. But there were certainly some bad mills – and bad masters.

B George Oldfield described life as a child in a Yorkshire mill in about 1842. (The account was written in 1904.)

We had to be up at 5 in the morning to get to the factory, ready to begin work at 6, then work [till] 8, when we stopped ½ an hour for breakfast, then work to 12 noon; for dinner we had 1 hour, then work [till] 4. We then had ½ an hour for tee, then commenced work again on to 8.30. If any time during the day had been lost, we had to work while 9 o'clock, and so on every night till it was all made up. Then we went to what was called home.

Many times I have been asleep when I had taken my last spoonful of porige – not even washed, we were so overworked and underfed. I used to curse the road we walked on.

C James Myles wrote about a factory incident in *Chapters in the Life of a Dundee Factory Boy* (1850). The event took place some years earlier.

One day [a boy] was carrying an armful of bobbins. He sat down to rest himself. In a few moments he was fast asleep.

The master happened to pass by. Without the least warning he gave him a violent slap on the side of the head, which stunned him. In a half-sleeping state he ran to the [machine] which he sometimes attended. Five minutes had barely passed when his left hand got entangled in the machinery. Two of his fingers were crushed to a jelly, and had to be immediately amputated.

A From *The History of the Cotton Manufacture of Great Britain* (1835). It shows a spinning mule, invented in 1779. Details of typical working conditions are printed opposite.

A typical day's work was 13-14 hours, with 4 hours on Sundays. The only holidays were Christmas Day and Good Friday. Overtime was common and often compulsory. Work sometimes continued through meal times. It was so noisy you had to lip read or use sign language. Temperatures were at least 60°-90°F (15°-32°C) in the spinning rooms. Piecers walked up to 27 miles (43 km) in a day.

D This picture appeared in a novel called *The Life and Adventures of Michael Armstrong, Factory Boy* (1840). Its writer was against child labour.

E Dr Andrew Ure: *The Philosophy of Manufactures* (1835).

Ill-treatment of any kind is very rare. I have visited many factories in Manchester and I never once saw a child [beaten]. Nor did I ever see children in ill-humour. [They] seemed to be always cheerful and alert. It was delightful to see the nimbleness with which they pieced the broken ends. They were delighted to show off their skill to a stranger. They showed no trace of [exhaustion] on emerging from the mill in the evening; they immediately began to skip about and to commence their little amusements, the same as boys issuing from a school.

F Nassau Senior gave his view in *Letters on the Factory Act* (1837).

The easiness of the labour [makes] long hours of work [possible]. [Most of] the work is merely that of watching the machinery, and piecing the threads that break. The work is scarcely equal to that of a shopman behind a counter in a [busy] shop.

G The Royal Commission on Factory Employment (1832) made this statement.

People in domestic manufacture are in most cases worked at an earlier age for longer hours and for less wages than children employed in factories.

H Working in a cotton factory.

These two pages include only a few sources about working in cotton mills. These sources can be used to produce two different views of factory life. The sources a historian chooses will affect how he or she interprets events.

1 a) Please work in pairs. Divide your page into columns like this:

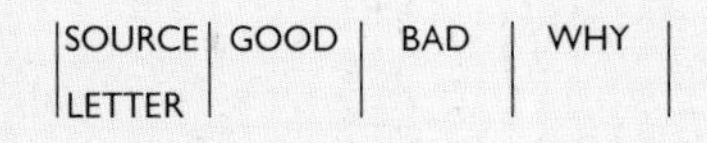

SOURCE LETTER	GOOD	BAD	WHY

Take each source in turn and decide whether it gives a good or bad view of factory work. Put a tick in either column 2 or 3. In column 3, briefly say how you decided.

b) Give each source a mark out of ten to show how reliable you think it is. (A completely reliable source would get ten marks.)

2 a) Now, one of you should write a brief account of factory life, using only the sources in column 2. The other should write a brief account, using only the sources in column 3.

b) How have your sources affected your interpretation of factory life?

3 a) In source A, what are workers 1 and 2 doing?

b) Compare sources A and D. How do they give different views of (i) the workers and (ii) the building?

c) Which picture do you think gives the more reliable idea of a factory? Give reasons.

FACTORY WORK AND FAMILY LIFE

A Children on their way to work in a Yorkshire factory (1814).

The new machinery and the factories were part of an industrial revolution. The changes were so great that they affected almost every aspect of life. It wasn't just a family's working life which changed: their home life changed, too.

Working at home, people had taken days off work whenever they felt like it. But factory workers chould not choose their own hours. The factory bell rang out in Cromford to tell people when work began and ended. Workers really hated the bells.

Before the arrival of factories, the family had lived and worked together. The children worked long hours, just as the factory children did. If they did not do their work, they were beaten, just as the factory children were beaten. In both situations, many children were underfed and often sick.

But there were differences. In the domestic system, children worked at home. When they were beaten, the slaps were given by their mother or father. And, of course, a young child's mother was usually never far away. The factory system changed all that.

Once the mother was working in a factory, she could not look after the young children. Either an older child stayed at home or the youngest children spent the day with a neighbour. Others were just locked in the house.

B Lord Shaftesbury described a mother's working day to Parliament in 1844. He was quoting a factory inspector.

Half an hour to dress and **suckle** her infant and carry it to [the] nurse; one hour for household duties before leaving home; half an hour for travelling to the mill; twelve hours' labour; one and a half hours for meals [at work]; half an hour for returning home at night; one and a half hours for household duties and preparing for bed.

Before the factory age, girls watched their mothers bring up the younger children. Now, the mothers were at work and so were the girls from four or five years upwards. They married young and began a family soon afterwards.

They probably didn't have the faintest idea how to bring up a baby. Few knew how to look after a home; some could not even cook. In any case, there was little time for cooking: during the week, many families made do with cold food, such as bread and cheese.

The daily meals of a cotton worker's family in 1833. They occasionally had meat, cheese and eggs.

D A reconstruction of a worker's home.

Pregnancy was a nuisance; it briefly stopped the mother from earning money. In Lancashire, women were usually back at work within two weeks of having a baby. We will never know how many women had abortions. But, as the children grew older, the parents showed more interest in them.

C This was what Charles Harris told a government enquiry in 1833:

I have a father and mother and give them what I earn. I have worked over-hours for two or three weeks together. We are paid for over-hours at the rate of 2d (less than 1p) for three hours. I always have that for myself.

At the end of the day, the children sometimes fell asleep on the floor. Often, they were too tired to eat. Their mothers and elder sisters often worked at nights. One factory-owner said that the beds in Lancashire never got cold.

However, factory work at least made an unmarried woman independent. She was able to earn her own wage so she was not forced into getting married young. Even married women were better off in the long run: under the domestic system, they could only earn what their husbands chose to give them.

The industrial revolution increased British trade and made the nation rich. The changes resulted in great economic progress, However, changes do not always bring progress. Historians must judge whether anything regressed (grew worse) as a result of the industrial revolution.

1 a) How was factory work different from working at home?
b) In what ways was it the same for the children?
c) Which change do you think workers most disliked? Explain how you decided.

2 a) Read source B carefully. Assume that this woman got up at 6 am in the morning. Write down what she did during the day and put the times beside each event. For example – 6.00-6.30 am: dressed and looked after infant.
b) Add up the hours she spent. How much free time did she have left?

3 If both parents worked in a factory, was life better or worse for (a) the mother, (b) the children and (c) babies? In each case, give reasons for your answer.

3 STEAM POWER

1750 1775 1800 1825 1850 1875 1900

The early cotton mills were powered by water because it was the best form of power they had – but it was not perfect. In summer, the stream might dry up; in winter, it might freeze over. If either of these things happened, the mill had to shut. The mill-owners needed something more reliable to power their mills.

Steam was already being used to pump water out of mines. Thomas Newcomen had invented a steam pump in 1708. However, his engines used a lot of coal: 80 per cent of the energy they produced was wasted. In any case, they could only produce an up-and-down motion: this was no use for making factory machines work.

A *Children's Encyclopaedia* (about 1950).

The mind of a true genius had yet to arrive. It did arrive when James Watt was born at Greenock, in 1736. [The story is often told] of how the boy was [told off] for wasting his time looking at the kettle-lid rising and falling as the water boiled.

B A painting of the young James Watt studying a kettle (19th century).

In fact, James Watt was 27 before he began experimenting with steam engines. He had a workshop at Glasgow University and had been sent a model of one of Newcomen's engines to repair.

Watt admitted that he knew nothing about steam engines but he set to work and repaired it. Even so, it still did not work well. He later worked out what was wrong. The engine's cylinder was cooled by jets of cold water. Each time, it had to be reheated to push the piston up. He saw it would be better if the cylinder stayed hot.

Watt's solution was to make a second cylinder where the steam was condensed. This meant that the main cylinder did not have to be cooled. So power was not wasted.

Watt later said that 'the invention will not appear so great as it seems to be'. But he patented it in 1769 and, in 1774, he joined up with a Birmingham factory-owner called Matthew Boulton to make steam engines.

In 1781, Watt invented a rotary engine which could turn wheels. At last, steam power could be used in factories. The first rotary engine appeared in a spinning-mill in 1785. A water wheel might slow down or even stop. The new steam engine just kept going.

C Edward Baines explained why steam-powered looms were better than hand weaving in *The History of the Cotton Manufacture of Great Britain* (1835).

A very good handloom weaver, 25 or 30 years of age, will weave two pieces of [cloth] per week, each 24 yards long. In 1833, a power loom weaver, from 15 to 20 years of age, attending to four looms, can weave eighteen similar pieces in a week; some can weave twenty.

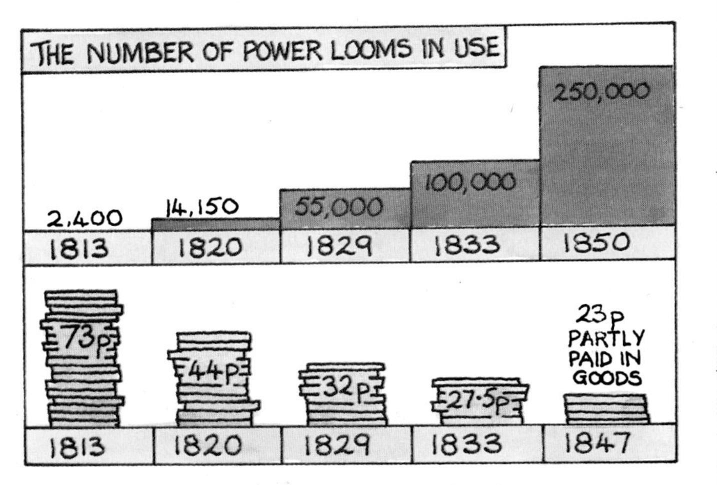

D The power loom was invented in 1785. Technical problems meant that it did not become common until the 1830s. The lower figures show what happened to the weekly earnings of home weavers.

E This 1830 cartoon shows the uses and results of steam power.

1 a) Write each of these dates on separate lines in chronological order: 1781; 1769; 1785; 1708; 1774.
b) Beside each, write down what happened in that year.

2 a) Read source A. Why is this story unlikely to be true?
b) Why do you think books print stories like this if they are not true?
c) How useful is source B for a historian studying the steam engine? Give reasons.

3 a) Look carefully at source E. What four goods are being made using steam power?
b) What results of steam power are shown at the numbered places?
c) Do you think the artist thought steam power was a good or bad thing? Give reasons.

4 This question is about the consequences of steam power.
a) Divide your page into three columns, headed 'technological', 'economic' and 'social'.
b) List as many results of steam power as you can in each column.
c) Which consequence do you think was most important for (i) mill-owners and (ii) workers? Give reasons.

KING COAL

A This is a reconstruction of a mining scene in a modern museum. Some seams were only 18 inches (45cm) high.

Even before Watt invented his steam engines, people needed coal. They used it in their homes. Industry also used it to make things like soap and bricks. Mining was a risky business but at least most pits were open to the air.

But Watt's steam engine had two effects. First, it increased the demand for coal. The answer was to dig down further to get it. Few pits in 1750 went deeper than 200ft (60m). As demand rose higher, so the pits went down deeper. By the 1830s, many mines were five times deeper.

Watt's engine actually helped to make this possible. It could pump water from far underground. But the deeper the mines went, the more dangerous a miner's job became. Apart from the risk of flooding, there was the chance of coming across dangerous gases. Carbon dioxide would make you choke. Methane could cause fires, set off by the miners' candles.

The safety lamp, invented by Sir Humphrey Davy in 1815, gave miners some protection: the light was surrounded by wire gauze so it could not cause explosions. Even so, miners often carried a canary to warn them of gas. The gas would kill the bird before it caused an explosion.

B Estimates of how coal production increased, 1750-1900.

Mining was a family business, as in the cloth industry. Men, women and children all took part. Even the children often saw daylight only on Sundays. But mining villages were often far away from major towns. So few people knew what working in a coal-mine was like.

In 1842, that all changed. Parliament published an enquiry into mining. For the first time, people found out what mine work was like – and they were shocked. In the Mines Act of 1842, Parliament banned women and children under ten from working underground.

Most people thought it was a step forward to prevent women and young children from doing this dangerous work. Some miners did not agree. About 2,000 women lost their jobs. Some were so keen to keep working that they dressed up as men to try and keep their jobs.

(Scènes dans les mines de houille, en Angleterre. — Le Trapper.)

C The youngest children, aged 5-10, were employed as trappers. They opened and closed the air-doors to let the corves through. Typical wages were 12p-20p a week.

Historians study consequences (results) of events. They do this by studying sources. All the sources on this page are taken from the Mines Report (1842). Witnesses giving evidence did not first have to swear an oath.

Historians must decide how useful each source is. To decide this, a historian asks two questions: (i) how reliable is the source and (ii) what information can be gained from it?

D Winding children up from a mine. The 1842 Act banned boys under 15 from doing this job.

E A Welsh boy trapper said:

I have been down in the pit since I was five. When I first went down I couldn't keep my eyes open. I don't fall asleep now; I smokes my pipe.

F S S Scriven visited nearly 200 pits to get evidence. He described the scene shown in source D.

In getting off you are at the mercy of the winder. The winder grabs your hand and brings you to land. David Pellett was drawn over the roller by his own uncle and grandfather, when their attention was drawn to a passing funeral.

Average wages in Bradford and Leeds mines in 1842.

G Girls and women, often naked to the waist, pushed or pulled the corves. Typical wages for a 17-year-old were 51p a week.

H Patience Kershaw, aged 17, said:

I go to the pit at five in the morning. I take my dinner with me, a cake, and eat as I go; I do not stop or rest any time. The bald place on my head is made by [pushing] the corves. I push the corves a mile or more and back. I am the only girl in the pit; there are 20 boys and 15 men; all the men are naked.

1. What were the consequences of these five changes? (Remember that a change may have more than one consequence.)
   a) the invention of Watt's steam engine;
   b) the demand for more coal;
   c) digging deeper pits;
   d) the invention of the safety lamp;
   e) the 1842 Mines Act.
2. a) Describe the work of a trapper, using sources C and E.
   b) Describe the work shown in source G. Use sources G and H to help you with your answer.
   c) Are pictures or written sources more useful for telling you about what the miners did? Give reasons.
   d) Which kind of source tells you most about working conditions? Again, give reasons.
3. a) Look at the pictures. What would you want to know about them to decide if they were reliable?
   b) How reliable do you think the written sources are? Give reasons.

4 CHANGE IN THE IRON INDUSTRY

1750 1775 1800 1825 1850 1875 1900

Water and steam provided the power for Britain's industrial revolution. Iron made the machine age possible. Machines had to be tough if they were powered by steam. Wooden ones were not strong enough.

Industry needed huge amounts of wrought iron. The man who made this possible was Henry Cort. In 1783, he patented a new process.

Pig iron was heated in a furnace while workers stirred it to get rid of the carbon in the iron. This was known as puddling. It was then hammered before going to the rolling mill, which was also invented by Henry Cort.

A A Boulton and Watt steam engine, made of iron.

B A rolling mill at the Cyfarthfa Works in Merthyr Tydfil. Cyfarthfa was the first ironworks to use the puddling process. The furnaces are on the right.

C The world's first iron bridge, built at Coalbrookdale, Shropshire in 1779.

Historians study changes in the past. There are many different kinds of changes. Cort's inventions brought *technological* changes to the iron industry. In turn, these caused *economic* change (to do with money) and *social* change (to do with how people lived and worked).

Industry needed coal and iron; Wales was rich in both. The Seven Years' War (1756-63) meant that cannon were needed in large numbers. So, rich Englishmen moved to South Wales with money to invest. The American War of Independence (1775-83) increased the demand for iron. By 1788, there were thirteen blast furnaces in Merthyr Tydfil alone.

The men who owned them were called ironmasters. Most famous of them all was Richard Crawshay. He became ironmaster at the Cyfarthfa Works in Merthyr Tydfil in 1794.

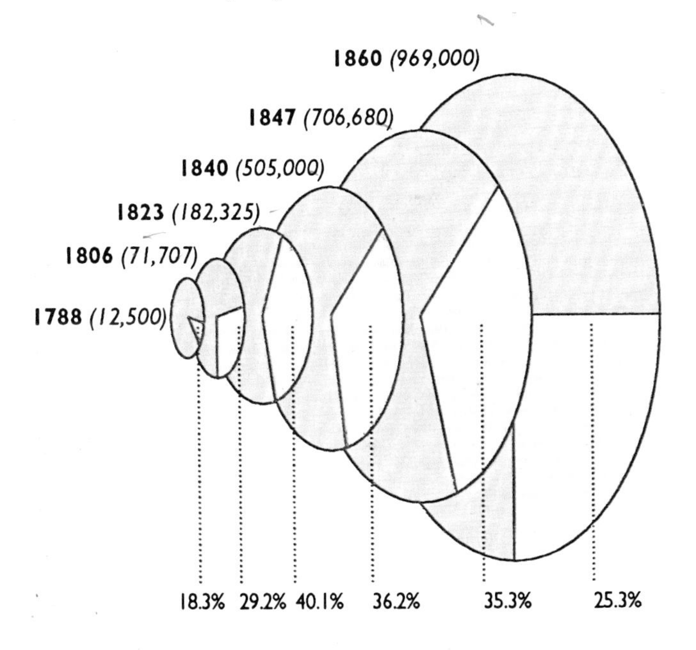

D The output of pig iron in South Wales, compared with total British production (in tons). The percentage figures show production in South Wales.

The new ironmasters faced various problems. Transport was one of them. Finding workers was the most urgent. There were just not enough people living in the area and those who did lacked the necessary skills.

The answer was to find workers elsewhere. At first, huge numbers of Welsh people moved from the countryside into the growing industrial towns of South Wales. They were joined by Irish immigrants. After 1850, most of the newcomers were English. As a result, the Welsh language was used less.

Merthyr Tydfil became a boom town of the 19th century. Ironmasters such as Crawshay became rich. When times were good, they paid fair wages, by the standards of the time. But when demand fell, so did wages. And, as in the coal mines, young children worked in dangerous conditions. A 12-year-old girl earned 15p a week for working 12 hours a day in 1841.

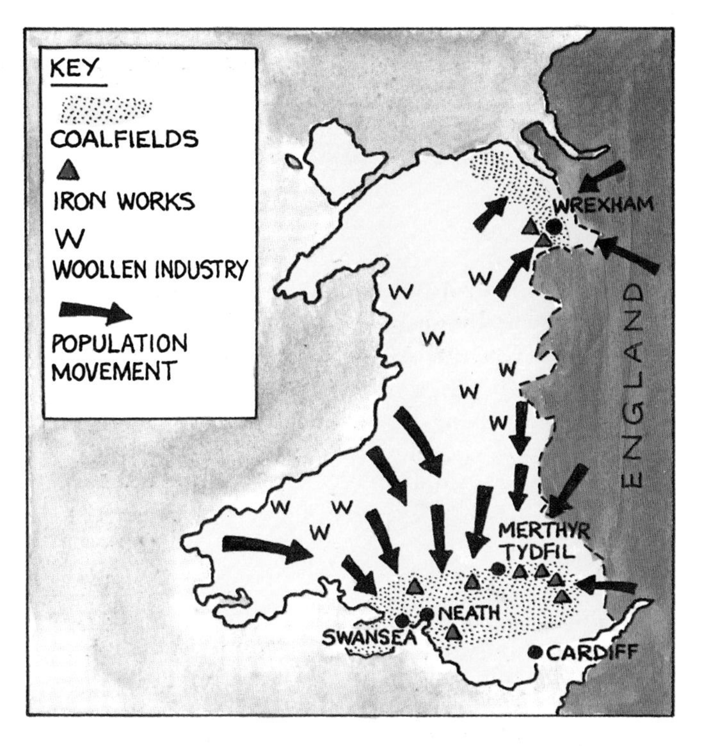

E The growth of the coal and iron industries in Wales.

Iron remained the key industry until the second half of the 19th century, after which steel began to take over. In 1855, Henry Bessemer patented a way of turning pig iron directly into steel. His new process was both quick and cheap – and other countries began developing their own steel industries. For Merthyr Tydfil's ironworks, the boom years were over.

1 a) Look at sources A and C on page 20. Could each object have been made entirely of wood? Give a reason.
b) Look carefully at source B. What can you see that is made of iron?

2 a) What technological changes are mentioned on these pages?
b) Write down at least one economic change caused by the iron industry.
c) Write down at least one social change caused by the iron industry.

3 a) Think carefully. Who benefited from the technological changes? Give as many people (or groups) as possible, with reasons why they benefited.
b) Look at all the changes. Choose one which you think brought benefits to the Welsh people. Explain why you chose it.
c) Now, choose one change which did not benefit the Welsh. Again, explain your choice.

5 HOUSES FOR THE WORKERS

In 1801, Merthyr Tydfil was still quite a small town with just 8,000 inhabitants. Fifty years later, the number had shot up to 46,000. People moved in from the countryside in search of work. Merthyr Tydfil was not unusual. Many British towns grew as fast, if not faster.

A How the population grew in various towns and cities. The figures for 1750 are estimates.

	1750	1801	1851
Glasgow	23,000	77,000	345,000
Manchester	18,000	75,000	303,000
Birmingham	24,000	71,000	233,000
Liverpool	35,000	82,000	376,000
Leeds	10,000	53,000	172,000
Newcastle	28,000	33,000	88,000

Of course, all these newcomers needed homes. There were no buses in 1801: the only way people could get to work was by walking. So workers needed homes close to the factory or mine.

The houses had to be built cheaply because the workers couldn't afford much rent. Land cost money. Builders wanted to build as many houses as possible on the smallest amount of land.

Many of the houses were probably no worse than homes in the middle ages but there were two great differences. First, there were simply far more of them, with more people living in them. Second, the fresh air of the countryside was no longer quite so close.

At first, there were few services. Landlords did not worry too much if the water supply was dirty; nor were they keen to pay to have cesspits emptied. As a result, a human dungheap might stand for months – or even years. In the meantime, the youngest children sometimes played on it.

In any case, going outside to the privy on a cold winter's night was not a pleasant experience. It was far easier to go indoors. People sometimes used an empty house as an indoor privy. One schoolteacher actually had to teach pupils how to use a privy: they did not know.

How a house could be built for just £50. Why would these houses have been unhealthy?

Each town had its own building style. Sunderland built single-storey terrace houses; Newcastle had two-storey flats. In Glasgow, they went in for tenements: tall blocks of flats, with up to seven storeys, as in source B. The drain ran down the centre of the street and everybody used the pump shown on the right.

B

E Some workers were lucky. The firm of J and J Cash built these houses for their ribbon-weavers in Coventry in about 1840. They are still standing today.

C A doctor described conditions in the Scottish town of Greenock (quoted in Chadwick's *Report*, 1842).

In one part of the town there is a dunghill – yet it is too large to be called a dunghill. It contains a hundred cubic yards of filth, collected from all parts of the town. It belongs to a person who deals in dung: he sells it by cartfuls. To please his customers, he always keeps it for some time before selling it. The older the filth is, the higher is the price.

The heap is beside a public street, enclosed by a wall. The height of the wall is about twelve feet [4 metres] and the dung overtops it: the filthy liquid oozes through the wall, and runs over the pavement. [In nearby houses,] all food and drink must be covered: if left for a minute, the flies at once attack it and it is made unfit for use, from the strong taste of the dunghill left by the flies.

D A contemporary writer said why conditions were bad.

These towns have been built by small **speculators** with no interest for anything except immediate profit. A carpenter and a brick-layer club together to buy a patch of ground, and cover it with what they call houses. In one place we saw a whole street following the course of a ditch, in order to have deeper cellars without the cost of [digging them].

It is rare for an event to have just one cause. The state of workers' housing from 1750 onwards had many causes. These causes are linked together, rather like a spider's web. The historian has to sort them out to find out what caused what.

1 Please work in pairs on scrap paper.

a) Listed below are some reasons why workers' housing was often so bad. Write each one on your paper, spread out around the sides. Then, read (b).

1 Towns grew fast between 1750 and 1850.
2 There was no public transport at first.
3 Many houses were needed quickly.
4 Builders wanted to make easy profits.
5 Land cost money.
6 People were ignorant about the causes of disease.

b) Write down at least one result (effect) of each statement.

c) Read the chapter again and write down any other causes of bad housing.

d) Using a pencil, draw arrows to link up causes and effects. Don't rush: some causes may cause other causes.

e) When you think you've got it right, draw the diagram in your book.

f) Afterwards, one pair should present their ideas to the class and you may discuss any differences.

PUBLIC HEALTH

In working-class areas of towns, disease spread fast. There was no proper sewage system, so dirt and germs often infected the water supply. By 1830, Liverpool had 11 miles (17km) of sewers but not one of them was built in a poor area.

Private water companies provided a water supply from pumps. However, water was only turned on for a few hours a day, often when the family was at work. The alternative was to buy water from the water carriers. It was usually filthy.

Much of this water came from a nearby river or canal. It was often the same river or canal into which people tipped their raw sewage. Along the River Thames, in Reading and Maidenhead, people used the river as a toilet. So did the people of London. Then, the people of London cooked with it. No wonder disease spread so fast.

Killer diseases included cholera, carried by infected water. It first swept through Britain in 1831-2. About half of those who caught it died. Doctors could do little to help. No one knew what caused cholera; many doctors believed it was spread by bad air. No one knew that germs caused disease until Louis Pasteur proved this in 1864.

However, by then, there had been progress. In 1849, Dr Snow of London suggested that cholera might be spread by dirty water. In 1854, another cholera outbreak in London gave him the chance to prove it. Even so, over 14,000 people still died of the disease as late as 1866.

Earlier, in 1842, Edwin Chadwick had published a report on workers' health. Many Victorians believed that the dreadful living conditions were caused by the workers themselves: they drank too much and they were just downright lazy. Many even thought that to be ill was a sin.

Chadwick disagreed. He believed that diseases were a main cause of poverty. They were caused, he said, by filth, raw sewage and dirty water. He wanted to improve the water and sewage systems. After all, he argued, if children died young, they could not work in factories; nor could men who were sick. Disease meant the country produced fewer goods; it was simply not good for business.

In 1848, Parliament passed the first Public Health Act. However, it only forced local councils to take action if the town had a very high death rate. It was 1875 before all towns were compelled to have a proper sewer system and water supply.

A A London slum of 1870. In one part of London, 13,000 people shared one water pump.

No.	When taken ill.	When died.	Where died.	Sex.	Age.	Occupation.	Circumstances.	Habits.	Any evidence of contagion or infection.	State of the Dwellings or Neighbourhood.
1	22nd August...	24th August ...	15, David square, Abercannaid	M.	36	Wife of Puddler ... (Welsh)	Very poor ..	Dirty	No possible contact ...	Damp, dirty, and unventilated.
2	22nd „ ...	25th „ ...	57, Quarry row, Tydfil's Well	F.	45	Wife of Fireman ... (Irish)	Poor	Dirty	ditto ...	Dirty, unventilated—yard at back most filthy.
3	23rd „ ...	25th „ ...	31, do do ...	M.	32	Fireman................ (Welsh)	Good	Clean and regular	ditto ...	A drain, which carries away house slops from houses above, runs under the house.
4	23rd „ ...	26th „ ...	13, Morris court, Merthyr	F.	75	Rag cleaner .... (Irish)	Poor	Clean	As a rag cleaner might have picked infected clothes	An untrapped gully at end of court, also heaps of ashes steeped with excrement, &c. House, no ventilation.
5	24th „ ...	25th „ ...	7, Cwm Canol street, Dowlais	M.	21	Hooker in Iron Mills (Irish)	Young Irish Labourer	Regular	No possible contact ...	Cesspool at back of house above level of lower floor—offensive.
6	24th „ ...	25th „ ...	1, Flag & Castle ct., Dowlais	M.	8	Son of Labourer ... (English)	Very poor ...	Dirty	ditto ...	Court unpaved, no convenience, earth sodden with house refuse.
7	24th „ ..	1st September	16, Sunny Bank, Tydfil's Well	F.	53	Wife of Tailor ...... (Welsh)	Very poor ...	Intemperate & Dirty	ditto ...	Cesspool in garden overflowing, floor of sleeping room thickly covered with dirt and filth.
8	25th „ ...	27th August ...	1, Miles' court, Caedraw	F.	50	Wife of Hawker ... (Scotch)	Poor	Clean and regular	Her husband and herself travelled about the neighbouring towns—had been in Aberdare	Cesspool near house overflowing.
9	26th „ ...	30th „ ...	8, Coffin's ct., George Town	F,	80	Wife of Skinner ... (Welsh)	Poor	Very clean ...	Had attended her son, case No. 3	Unventilated—common cesspool in gardens full.
10	27th „ ...	1st September	4, Lewis' square, Abercannaid	F.	32	Wife of Collier ...... (Welsh)	Comfortable .	Clean and regular	Apparently spontaneous	Overcrowded with family and lodgers—9 out of the 12 attacked, 7 died. At back of bedroom heap of ashes foul with excrement.
11	28th „ ...	1st „ ...	9, Sunny Bank	F.	42	Wife of Labourer ... (Irish)	Comfortable .	Clean	May have visited case No. 7	
12 13	3rd September 6th „ ...	5th „ 8th „	13, Mt. Pleasant, Penydarren	F. F,	21 8	Wife and Daughter of Collier (Welsh)	Comfortable .	Clean	No known contact ...	Unceiled cow shed under the house in a most filthy state.

B This is a list of some of those who died in a cholera outbreak in Merthyr Tydfil in 1866.

C The *Bath Chronicle* described conditions in a poor family's home in 1852.

The room was in a horrible state, and there were excrements all over the place. The two beds were black and shining with body grease. [The] bedding was stinking and rotten and covered with filth. On the bed was lying a little boy, naked except for a piece of cloth around its neck. [He was] thin, ill and apparently struggling for breath.

The child was sucking from a filthy feeding bottle which contained sour milk curds, while the teat was stinking. I swept maggots from under the bed with a broom. With the handle of the broom I stirred up maggots from the bed itself.

D This evidence about Liverpool was given to a government committee in 1840.

There is a great deal of broken ground, in which there are pits. At the fall of the year there is a good deal of water in them, in which there have been thrown dead dogs and cats. This water is nevertheless used for [cooking]. I could not believe this at first.

There is a good supply of water for the poor, if they had the means of preserving it. The water is turned on a certain number of hours during the day – four hours, perhaps. Each person fetches as much as they have pans to receive; but they are not well supplied with these articles, [so] they are frequently out of water.

Historians never rely on just one source. They study different sources and compare them. Two primary sources may be useful – but for different purposes.

1 a) What evidence of poverty can you see in source A?
b) Would this area be suitable for children to play in or not? Give reasons.

2 a) Study source B carefully. How can you tell that cholera killed both the old and the young?
b) In how many cases was the house or the area outside dirty?
c) Be careful. How useful is source B for telling us why people caught cholera?

3 a) Read sources C and D. Using both sources, explain why poor people were likely to be ill.
b) Which of these sources is more useful for understanding why cholera spread? Explain how you decided.

4 Design a poster to warn people about cholera after 1854, when the cause of the disease was known. It must be suitable for people who cannot read and must have a dramatic effect.

6 ART AND ARCHITECTURE

1750 1775 1800 1825 1850 1875 1900

The industrial revolution affected people's lives in every way possible. Architecture was no exception. In the past, each part of the country had its own styles of building, using local materials.

The industrial revolution brought factories – and factories brought mass production. The invention of railways meant that the same sort of cheap brick and slate could be used anywhere. Building, too, became a system of mass production, using the cheapest materials. The workers' slum houses were one result.

Of course, the rich could afford to build what they liked, using the very best materials. And what the rich of the 19th century wanted to do was to show others how rich they were. So the first thing which many of them did was to knock down the old manor houses and build something bigger.

You might have expected the new buildings to have been built in a new style. Usually, they were not. Victorian architects copied styles from the past. The main fashion of the time was to build in the **Gothic** style. It had first been popular in the 13th and 14th centuries.

A Although it was built at the beginning of the 20th century, around 1910, Castle Drogo in Devon was still made to look like a fake castle.

In a way, it was odd that the Victorians copied earlier styles because the industrial revolution provided huge amounts of cheap iron. After about 1860, there was plenty of steel, too. These metals made it possible to build higher arches than ever before.

Glass, too, was easily available: whole roofs and walls could be made of it. At the end of the 19th century, reinforced concrete was introduced. Why were these not being used to create new and different buildings?

The answer is that they were – but mainly by engineers, not by architects. Source B shows Paddington Station in London; it was designed by railway engineer Isambard Kingdom Brunel.

B

Artists, too, were influenced by the industrial revolution. Of course, artists must earn a living: someone must actually buy their paintings. So, in the 18th century, there were few paintings of ordinary workers – but there *were* paintings and prints of early factories.

People were proud of these new buildings. They provided jobs for the poor; they brought wealth to the country. So, the paintings often made the factories look impressive. Fifty years later, attitudes were changing. People had a better idea of how bad working in a factory could be.

C *The Iron Forge*, painted in 1779.

Artists and writers reflected these changing views. Some people preferred to ignore reality; they were happier looking back to an earlier age, before the industrial revolution. Others became sentimental about industry and those who worked in it.

D *Coalbrookdale at Night*, a painting of about 1800. Here, in 1709, Abraham Darby had discovered how to smelt iron ore using coke.

But there were those who took a different view. In recent years, there have been many films about the monster created by Dr Frankenstein. He first appeared in a book called *Frankenstein*, published in 1817. In the book, a clever doctor created a monster which got out of control. This was what some people thought had happened to industry.

1 a) Look at source A. How is this like a castle?
b) Why would a wealthy person in the 19th century want to build a home looking like a castle?

2 Look at source C. Remember that this is *inside* a forge.
a) Describe the woman's clothes and the man's pose.
b) Why do you think the painter has shown them like this?
c) How realistic do you think this picture is? Explain your answer carefully.
d) Even if it's not realistic, what can a historian learn from it?

3 a) How did people's attitudes change towards factories?
b) Why did they change?
c) Look at source D. What do you think this painter's attitude was towards the ironworks? Explain how you decided.

7 BETTER TRANSPORT

A Yorkshire road menders, working on a turnpike road (1814).

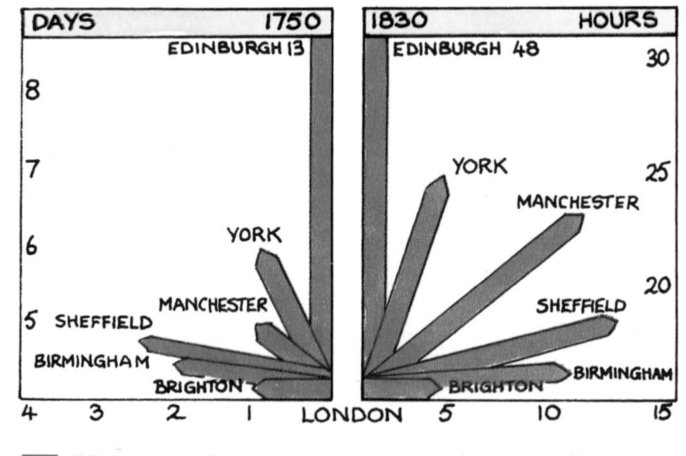

B How travel times improved between 1750 and 1830.

More industry meant that more goods were moved across the country. Yet, in 1750, many roads were in a worse state than they had been during Roman times. Most roads were just beaten mud tracks. There were no councils to repair roads, as there are today. Instead, the villagers did it. Each villager spent six days each year repairing the roads which ran through their village.

It was unpaid work and very unpopular; few cared about making good repairs; even fewer actually knew how to do it. Too often, stones were just piled in the holes and it was left at that. When wet weather came, you can guess what happened.

These roads were hardly fit to cope with the traffic before the industrial revolution. The furthest that goods could travel in a day was about 15 miles (24km). Manufacturers needed to be certain that their goods would arrive on time. But that was impossible; they couldn't even be sure they would arrive at all.

The government's answer was to let groups of people build better roads if they wished. Each group raised money to form a Turnpike Trust. The Trust then got Parliament's permission to improve a road, using the money it had raised.

Of course, each Trust needed to earn money to keep its road in good repair. It got this money by putting gates (turnpikes) along the road and charging people a toll (tax) to go through them.

By 1750, most of the main roads leading out of London had been turnpiked. By 1800, most major roads in the land were turnpike roads. The best roads were built by one of the great engineers: John McAdam invented a better, harder-wearing surface, while Thomas Telford built over 120 bridges for 900 miles (1,448km) of Scottish roads.

These were fine for passengers. But they did not really solve all the transport problems of industry. In 1820, less than one-fifth of public roads were run by turnpike trusts. The rest were still repaired by villagers or by paupers. They were as bad as ever. And even turnpike roads were not ideal for sending large amounts of bulky goods.

C On the road, goods were carried by wagon and horses, like the one above.

D Mail coaches were just one result of the building of turnpikes. After 1800, 370 towns had a daily postal service. This is the Devonshire mail coach (1840). It also carried passengers.

E A German count visited England in 1761. He described the Harwich-London turnpike in his diary (1761).

The broad road along which we drove is as even and well-kept as our [finest road]. The roads are always kept in good order with course or fine gravel or sand. The slightest unevenness is mended at once. The broad wheels of the carts and vans, which measure [23cm] wide, act as rollers to level the ruts cut by the other carriages.

F Adam Walker gave this judgement when he produced his *Report on Highways* (1808).

Examining the turnpike roads [near] London, I find the materials by which they are repaired seldom last longer than a month or six weeks in winter. [Then,] they are ground to atoms and raked off the road as puddle. In some places the tolls have been doubled yet the roads [are] sometimes almost impassable.

1 a) Look at source D. What jobs would have been created at the four places named on the picture? (There is more than one job at some of them.)
b) How did mail coaches help manufacturers?

2 a) Read sources E and F. What differences did these writers find?
b) Suggest a reason for the differences.

3 a) Look at source B. The distance from York to London is about 200 miles. At what speed did the coaches travel in 1830?
b) It cost about 3p to travel 4 miles inside a coach. What sort of people do you think made most use of coaches? Explain how you decided.

4 a) Why did manufacturers need better roads? Write down all the reasons you can think of.
b) Look at this statement. 'Turnpike roads solved the transport problems of industry.' Do you agree? Give your answer in two or three paragraphs.

CANALS

A The Bridgewater warehouse beside the Duke of Bridgewater's first canal.

The government mostly left it to individuals to build the roads of Britain; it was the same with canals. Although roads improved after 1750, it was still difficult to move heavy loads for long distances.

The mine owners knew this better than anyone. One of them was the Duke of Bridgewater who owned coal-mines at Worsley, 7 miles (11km) from Manchester. It cost the Duke up to 50p a ton to have his coal carried on horseback. It was expensive and it was slow.

In 1759, he asked an engineer to plan a canal from his mines to Manchester. They were an unlikely pair: the engineer, James Brindley, could hardly read or write. If he had a problem, he would go to bed to think about it and sort it out.

As for the Duke, his family believed he was simple-minded; they had thought of stopping him from inheriting his estate. But he was a clever businessman who knew what his problem was – and how he wanted to solve it. Brindley was clever enough to put the solution into practice.

B In about 1800, engineers carried out experiments to see what loads could be carried. These were the results.

When the canal was finished in 1761 it was an immediate success. The cost of transporting coal was cut by half. In 1772, the Duke opened his second canal, linking Manchester and Liverpool. It, too, cut transport costs by 50 per cent.

Other mine owners quickly saw the advantages. In fact, anyone with heavy goods could see that it was a cheaper, quicker way to get them to buyers. For instance, canals were ideal for farmers supplying the large towns with food. And for manufacturers of fragile goods, such as pottery.

A network of canals was built across the country: towns, ports and rivers were all linked up. These canals allowed manufacturers to sell their goods throughout Britain. At the same time, costs were cut.

But each canal was built by a different company. So, the canals varied in both width and depth; only a 20-ton boat could travel over the whole system. The barges were all horse-drawn; when steam power arrived, most canals did not have strong enough banks to cope with the wash a steam boat would create.

Yet it is easy to look back and find fault with Britain's canals. At the time, they gave manufacturers the best transport they had ever had. Well into the 1830s, many investors were getting huge dividends from canal shares. Few of them guessed that a better form of transport was about to drive many of them out of business.

Three new occupations came into being as a result of the canals.

C The writer Charles Dickens described life for a bargee's children in 1858:

On family barges there is a boatman and his wife and children, varying in number from two to ten, and in ages from three weeks to twelve years.

The youngest of these helpless little ones, dirty, ragged and stunted in growth, are confined in the cabin, stuck round the bed; sitting upon the cabin seat; standing in pans and tubs; rolling helplessly on the floor; lying on the poop, with no barrier to protect them from being shaken into the canal; always being scuffed and scolded; sickly, even under their sunburnt skins.

[They are] waiting wearily for the time when their little limbs will be strong enough to trot along the towing path; or dropping suddenly over the sides of the boat, quietly into the open, hungry arms of death.

When these helpless creatures reach five or six years of age they are [given] a whip, as drivers of the horse that tows the boat. Not a week passes but one of these canal-children is drowned.

D The official Inspector of Canal Boats gave his view in 1905.

The boat child is [mostly] superior to the land child in a similar [class]. Its open air life [makes it used] to all weathers. Work from an early age makes it reliant and strong.

On the boats, boys and girls can be found doing their work in a quiet way and taking a pride in doing it; [their] contemporaries ashore are a worry to their parents.

E A family on their canal barge.

1 This question is about causes and motives.
a) Why did the Duke of Bridgewater want a canal built?
b) Why did pottery manufacturers need canals?
c) Why do you think farmers were pleased to use canals?
d) Why do you think people wanted to invest in canals?
e) What do you think was the main cause of canal-building? Explain how you decided.
f) How were the different causes linked up? Please give a detailed answer.

2 a) How do the writers of sources C and D disagree? Answer in detail.
b) Which one do you think is more reliable? Give reasons.
c) Does that mean that the other source is of no use as evidence? Explain your answer.

RAILWAYS

A Richard Trevithick built the first steam locomotive to run on rails in 1804. In 1808, he took this one to London and gave rides to the public for 5p.

Coal had been the reason for the Bridgewater Canal – and coal was the reason for railways. The first ones appeared around 1600 to take coal from the pits to a river or the sea. These were not steam railways. The coal was put in wagons and pulled by horses along wooden rails.

In the early 19th century, people began experimenting with steam engines. One of them was a miner's son called George Stephenson. In 1821, when mine owners planned a railway from Stockton to Darlington, they made him their engineer.

The railway was built to carry coal to the port of Stockton. But, on the opening day, a steam locomotive pulled a train which had passengers on board. So, it became the world's first steam railway to carry passengers, although horse-drawn trains were still used for some years afterwards.

Stephenson went on to become engineer on the Liverpool to Manchester Railway, opened in 1830. This was the first real mainline railway; all its trains were pulled by steam engines. It was faster than travelling by stagecoach; it was cheaper than sending goods by canal: it was a success. The railway age had begun.

Railways were paid for by private investors, just as the roads and canals had been. As a result, the British railway system was quite unlike that of other countries. In France and Germany, the governments helped to pay for railways. They wanted to use them for military purposes.

So other countries got a railway network which was planned. Britain got one which grew up in a haphazard way. The government was keen to encourage competition. So each railway company planned its own routes. There was no central planning; as a result, there was no real system.

Parliament's attitude had one other effect. Each company built its line in the way it wished. Stephenson used a **gauge** of 4ft 8½ ins (143cm). But in Ireland, the gauge was 5ft 3ins (160cm). The Great Western Railway, from London to Bristol, used a gauge of 7ft (213cm). Its engineer, Isambard Kingdom Brunel, said it led to faster and more comfortable travel.

It was 1846 before Parliament accepted that one gauge was needed to avoid confusion. It chose 4ft 8½ins as the standard gauge. It is still the gauge used on British railways today.

B A painting of a first-class carriage in about 1830.

Historians try to understand how people at the time thought about events. This is really very difficult because each human being thinks in a different way. However, we need to understand people's attitudes to the early railways. These explain why there was so much opposition.

C The opening of the Stockton and Darlington Railway in 1825, from a sketch made some time afterwards.

D An Act of Parliament was needed before a railway could be built – and there was plenty of opposition. J Francis's *History of the English Railway* (1851) listed some objections to the Liverpool and Manchester Railway.

What was to become of the coach-makers and harness-makers, coach-masters, coach-men, inn-keepers, horse-breakers and horse-dealers? The beauty and comfort of country gentlemen's estates would be destroyed by it.

Was the House [of Commons] aware of the smoke and noise and the hiss which locomotives passing at ten or twelve miles an hour would [cause]? Iron would [go up] in price 100 per cent or more or would [run out] altogether. It would be the greatest nuisance that man could invent . . .

The country gentleman was told that the smoke would kill the birds as they passed over the locomotive. The public were told that the weight of the engine would [stop] it moving; the manufacturer was told that the sparks from its chimney would burn his goods. Elderly gentlemen were tortured with the [idea] that they would be run over. Ladies were alarmed at the thought that their horses would take fright. Cows, it was said, would cease to [give] milk.

E Sir J Macdonald wrote about early rail travel in *Life Jottings of an Old Edinburgh Citizen* (1918).

There were thousands who vowed that they would never put a foot in a railway carriage. A few of them never did.

What many people thought is shown by a scene when my stepmother [first travelled by train]. She had her handkerchief tightly pressed to her eyes and begged us not to make her uncover them. A more **abject** picture of terror I never saw.

Four years after this I went on a journey with her and all the fear was gone, and she should laugh like others.

1. Put these events in chronological order.
   (a) the standard gauge was chosen;
   (b) the Liverpool and Manchester Railway opened;
   (c) the Stockton and Darlington Railway opened;
   (d) Trevithick gave public rides in London.
2. a) Read source E. You are the stepmother about to travel by train for the first time. Write a postcard about it to a friend.
   b) Now, write a postcard after the later journey.
   c) What does this exercise teach you about people's attitudes?
3. Please work in pairs. Read source D. Pick any one of the objections. One of you should design a poster warning people of this risk. The other should design a poster for the railway company, explaining that there is no risk.

CONSEQUENCES OF THE RAILWAYS

A Train travel encouraged people to read. The railways also meant that national newspapers and letters could be taken anywhere in Britain (1862).

By 1850, there were over 6,500 miles (10,600 km) of railway track. For the next 50 years, branch lines were added to the main routes and lines were built into remote areas. The consequences were enormous. Almost every aspect of life was affected by the railways.

Stage coaches were the first to suffer. In 1850, fast trains travelled more than three times faster than a stage coach: the last stage coach had left London in 1846. Coach companies went out of business; turnpike trusts went bankrupt.

B

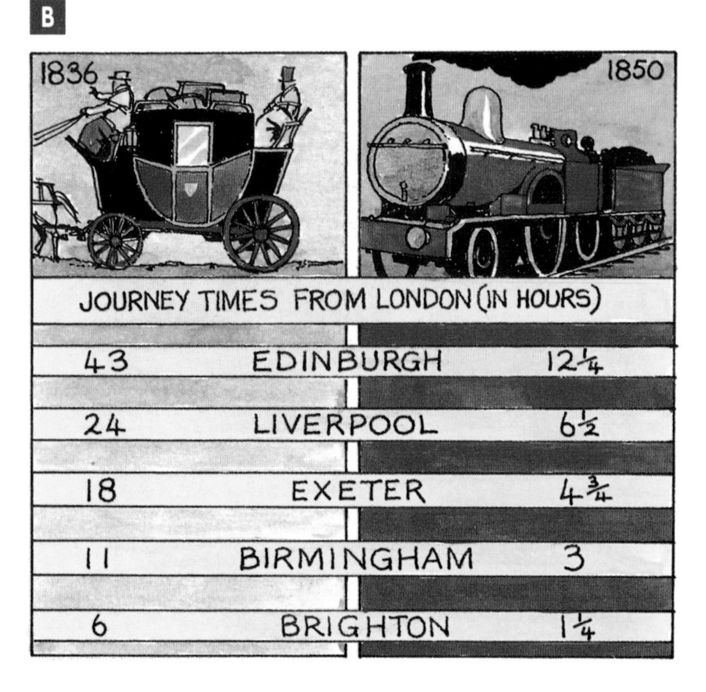

1836	JOURNEY TIMES FROM LONDON (IN HOURS)	1850
43	EDINBURGH	12¼
24	LIVERPOOL	6½
18	EXETER	4¾
11	BIRMINGHAM	3
6	BRIGHTON	1¼

The canal companies put up a better fight but manufacturers could now choose whether to send goods by canal or rail. In 1850, a train could carry twenty times the amount that a canal barge could carry – and up to eight times faster. Canal companies cut prices to try and survive. In the end, the competition killed them.

But other industries benefited from the railways. Stations, rails and the trains themselves all needed huge amounts of iron and, later, steel. The engines burned coal. As a result, many new jobs were created in these industries.

In addition, there were thousands of new jobs, building the railways and running them. Some towns grew rapidly because of the railways. Each company needed repair sheds and depots. The Grand Junction Railway built a model town for its workers at Crewe; the Great Western Railway did the same at Swindon.

C Swindon in about 1850 showing the houses and church built for the railway workers.

The railways bought up huge areas to use for all the buildings and sidings. Houses were knocked down – and those remaining were even more overcrowded.

For safety reasons, the railways needed a method of communication which was faster than the trains themselves. In 1837, two British scientists invented a telegraph system. Electric signals passed along wires which were set up beside the railway lines. Even the police benefited: in 1845, they arrested a murderer because they received a telegraph message before his train arrived.

D For the first time, even poor people could travel long distances. The working class made day trips from the industrial cities to Blackpool and Scarborough. Some south coast villages grew into seaside resorts because of the railway.

E J Ritchie from Suffolk recalled how the railways affected his area (1893):

I am old enough to remember how [peaceful] was the country, how stay-at-home were the people, what a sensation there was when anyone went to London, or any stranger appeared in our midst.

From afar we heard of railways, then we had a railway opened from London to Brentford; then the railways spread all over the land. The turnpikes were deserted; the inns were empty of customers; no longer did the villagers hasten to see the coach change horses, and the bugle of the guard was heard no more.

F Fast trains meant that fresh fish could be carried further inland. Fish and chips began replacing pigs' trotters as a cheap working-class supper. Farmers, too, benefited. This song celebrated the opening of the Oxford Railway (1852).

When it's finished at both ends
You may send your cocks and hens
And go and visit all your friends
With ducks and pigs and turkeys.
To any part wherever you please
You may send your butter and eggs
And they can ride who've got no legs
Along the Oxford Railway.

G Each part of the country had its own time when the first railways were built. It caused such confusion that station clocks began using London time. In 1880, Greenwich Mean Time became everyone's time in Britain.

The railways had many different consequences. Some affected how people lived (social consequences); others affected the wealth of the country (economic consequences); the railways also led to new inventions (technological consequences). Historians have to sort these out and decide which were the most important.

1 a) List all the changes which the railways brought about.
b) Think carefully. Did anyone suffer as a result of railway development? Explain your answer.

2 Divide your page into three columns. Put these headings at the top of your columns: Social, Economic and Technological. Under each heading, write down those consequences which you think fit in that column. (You may put a consequence in two columns, if you wish.)

3 a) Which social consequence do you think most affected people's lives? Explain how you decided.
b) What do you think was the most important consequence for (i) farmers, (ii) the working class and (iii) the government? Give reasons for your choices.

8 PROTEST AND REFORM

There was great poverty in the 1790s and 1800s. This picture shows two reasons why.

The new factory machines brought wealth to the mill-owners and problems for the workers. The hand workers could not compete with goods which were mass-produced on factory machines. Poverty forced many to go to work in factories.

But some workers thought that violence was the solution. The factories threatened their jobs; the machines were taking away their livelihood. Perhaps the answer was to burn down the factories and smash up the machines. Arkwright was one of the first victims. His mill at Chorley had been destroyed in the 1770s.

Events like these often happened suddenly, without much warning. However, a planned campaign of violence began in 1811. The gangs called themselves Luddites after an apprentice called Ned Ludd. People said that he lived in Sherwood Forest but the chances are that he did not exist at all.

In the spring of 1811, the stocking makers of Nottinghamshire began the Luddite attacks. Employers had begun using wide frames to make cheap stockings and the stocking knitters smashed up over 1,000 of them. The following year, the handloom weavers of Lancashire and Cheshire destroyed power looms in the mills; in Yorkshire, the target was shearing machines.

The government used harsh measures to stop the violence. In 1812, machine-breaking became a capital crime. Anyone found guilty was hanged. One 16-year-old was hanged just for acting as a sentry while his brothers destroyed a factory.

Similar violence occurred in the countryside in 1830. Farmers had been buying the new threshing machines. These meant that farmers did not need to employ so many workers over the winter. There was no unemployment pay in those days: many families risked starving to death.

Many of them, too, thought the answer lay in violence. They burned down hay ricks and barns; they smashed up the threshing machines. They sent threatening letters, signed 'Captain Swing'. Like Ned Ludd, it is unlikely that this person existed. However, like the Luddites, the Swing rioters were firmly dealt with. Nineteen of them were hanged, mostly for arson.

The Luddite attacks and Swing riots tried to stop industry using new machinery. Each tried to stop progress in technology; in the long run, each failed.

A This cartoon of 1844 was called *The Home of the Rick-burner*.

B Three Yorkshire Luddites were hanged in 1813 for their part in the violence. This reconstruction was made for a television programme (1988).

Why did the Luddites destroy machines?

C This source is taken from a school textbook (1987).

There were many new inventions at this time. This meant that many people lost their job. Some people tried to turn the clock back and destroyed the new machines. They hoped to return to their old way of life.

D G D H Cole and Raymond Postgate explained why violence broke out in Nottinghamshire in *The Common People* (1956).

In Nottinghamshire the Luddite campaign was not directed against new machinery but against the abuse of old machinery. The framework knitters had found their livelihood half-ruined by the war [against Napoleon]. On top of this, their condition was sharply worsened by the selling of 'cut-ups' made on wide frames.

Unscrupulous owners had their weavers weave large pieces of cloth on the wide frames and then cut the pieces by scissors into whatever [shape] it might be. These 'cut-ups' were then stitched up [and] rapidly fell to pieces. But the shoddy was ruining the market. The Luddites appeared in village after village and smashed the wide frames. A good many of the masters, though they did not approve of the methods, approved of the results.

E The *Leeds Mercury* reported in 1812:

They broke only the frames of [those who] have reduced the price of men's wages. In one house, last night, they broke four frames out of six; the other two belonged to masters who had not lowered their wages [and] they did not meddle with [them].

F Luddites destroying a machine. This is another scene from the 1988 television programme.

1 a) Look carefully at source A. Describe the condition of the family.
b) What link is the cartoonist suggesting between their condition and rick-burning? Explain your answer carefully.
c) What can a historian learn from source A?

2 a) Read sources C and D. How do the two writers disagree? Quote from the sources in your answer.
b) Which one is more useful for someone studying the reasons for the Luddite campaign? Explain how you decided.
c) How does source E add to your understanding of the Luddites?

3 a) Which sources on these two pages do you think are least reliable? Give reasons.
b) Give a detailed answer to this question. Why is it difficult to explain what caused the Luddites' violence?

PARLIAMENT BEFORE REFORM

A In 1819, a protest meeting at St Peter's Fields, Manchester, demanded the vote for workers. Mounted troops broke up the meeting and 11 people died.

Some workers believed that their lives would improve only when they were allowed to vote in elections. If they could vote, they could influence Parliament. If they could influence Parliament, MPs might try harder to make sure that workers had jobs. If workers had jobs, they could afford to buy bread.

In 1750, very few adults had the right to vote. In most areas, only property owners could vote. So the workers had little say in choosing MPs. Parliament was run by the landowners.

Each area which elects an MP is called a constituency. On average, there were just over 700 voters for each constituency. But this *was* just an average. For instance, Manchester was not big enough in 1750 to elect its own MP. By 1830, it had 182,000 inhabitants – but it still had no MP.

On the other hand, some towns had grown smaller over the years but still had two MPs to represent them. They were known as 'rotten boroughs'. By 1830, Old Sarum in Wiltshire was no more than a windy hilltop. Yet, each election day, a tent was put up and seven voters met to choose their two MPs. At Gatton in Surrey, it was even easier. There was just one voter.

In many other boroughs, everyone knew who would win the election. Most voters worked for a local landowner or else they rented land from him. They voted for the person he told them to vote for. Over 200 of the MPs were elected in this way. Lord Lonsdale alone chose nine of them.

In constituencies where there were hundreds or thousands of voters, there might be a proper election, with a choice of candidates. But the fairness went no further than that. The reason was that people voted in public. Each voter had to announce whom he was voting for. While an official wrote this down, other people might shout out abuse – or even pelt the voter with rotten fruit.

As a result, people could sell their votes to the highest bidder. In Liverpool in 1830, the price reached £150 per vote towards the end of the election. And the corruption did not end there, as the sources show.

B George Selwyn MP described the election at Gloucester in 1761. His opponent was Mr Snell.

Two of my voters were murdered yesterday by an experiment which we call shopping. [This is] locking them up and keeping them dead drunk until the day of the election. Mr Snell's agents forced two [of them] into a post-chaise where [they were] suffocated with brandy and a very fat man that had custody of them. They were taken out stone dead.

C Lord Fitzwilliam's representative wrote about events at the East Retford election in 1826.

Some men have been nearly killed by a hired mob of the scum of the neighbourhood, no doubt hired by our opponents. It is expected 20,000 persons will be spectators at the election. They not only threaten to block up the road to prevent the candidates coming into the hall, but murder freemen that vote for Roman Catholics. The freemen have every reason to expect their lives will be in danger if they go to vote; they cannot now walk the streets (even in daytime) without insult.

D Sir Philip Francis wrote about how he became MP for Appleby in 1802.

I was elected by [the] one elector. There was no other Candidate, no Opposition, no Poll demanded. So I had nothing to do but to thank the Elector for [choosing me].

E This cartoon shows William Pitt's supporters asking for bribes after the 1788 election.

Sources A and E contain a lot of useful information if you study them carefully. The glossary on page 80 will help you. However, a historian never relies on a single source. He or she takes information from various sources and uses it in their account of the past.

1. a) What is happening in source A?
   b) Write down at least one thing the protesters were demanding. (Write more, if possible.)
   c) Study the source carefully. How did the artist feel about this event? Explain how you know.
   d) Do you think this source is reliable or not? Explain how you decided.
2. a) Look at the numbered places in source E. Why were these four people being bribed? Please answer in your own words.
   b) Of all the sources, which one do you think is most useful for understanding why only rich people could become MPs? Explain how you decided.
3. a) Write at least two paragraphs to describe how candidates could win an election. Use sources B, C, D and E, as well as the text.
   b) Write at least two paragraphs to explain why MPs mainly represented the rich.

REFORMING PARLIAMENT

Whigs and Tories – the two main political groups.

Members of Parliament were mostly grouped into two parties – the Whigs and the Tories. Neither represented the working class. But the Whigs at least realised that England had changed since 1750. The Tories, by and large, did not. The difference is summed up by these two sources.

A Lord Brougham, a Whig, said:
We don't live in the days of Barons – we live in the days of Leeds, Bradford, Halifax and Huddersfield. We live in the days when men desire to be free.

B The Duke of Newcastle, a Tory, said:
My boroughs are mine to do what I like with.

However, change was on the way. In 1828, nonconformists were allowed to become MPs. In 1829, Roman Catholics were given the same right. By then, many people were convinced that Parliament itself had to be reformed.

By 1831, the Whigs had come to the same conclusion. But the only way to change Parliament was to pass an Act of Parliament – and the only people who could do that were the MPs. In other words, the MPs would have to vote some of themselves out of a job.

In 1831 the Whigs introduced a Reform Bill in the House of Commons. If it became law, 86 boroughs would lose one MP or both of them. In return, some new constituencies would be created, including 14 in industrial areas.

How important was this change?

C Peter Lane took this view in *Elections* (1973).
It became clear that really the proposed changes were minor indeed. [It] did not do away with tiny boroughs altogether – Reigate had only 152 [voters but] Tower Hamlets, in London, had over 7000 voters. Huddersfield and Rochdale [now had MPs but] most MPs continued to be elected by people in the South and West of the country.

D L F Hobley wrote this in *Living and Working* (1964).
The Bill went much further than many people had expected. Besides giving seats to the industrial towns, it extended the franchise to most of the middle class in the towns and to a great many farmers. Workers in town and country and smallholders were not enfranchised. Voting was not to be by ballot.

Historians often hold different views of the past. When reading secondary sources (such as this book), one of the first things that the reader must do is sort out facts from opinions. At the same time, the reader must check the facts.

1 a) Read sources C and D. How do they disagree?
b) Write down one opinion from each source. In each case, explain how you know that it's not a fact.
c) Think carefully. Source D says that the Bill gave 'seats to the industrial towns'. Does this agree with the text or not? Explain your answer.

In fact, the Reform Bill was rejected twice – first by the House of Commons and, later, by the House of Lords. That autumn, Britain came close to revolution. There were riots in many cities; in London, the Duke of Wellington's home was stoned by a mob; the Duke of Newcastle was assaulted.

So the Prime Minister, Lord Grey, tried again in December. For the second time, the House of Lords voted against the bill. Lord Grey resigned and King William IV tried to get the Tories to form a government. When they failed to get enough support, the king made Lord Grey Prime Minister once more. This time, the king promised that he would create enough new Whig peers to guarantee they would win the vote in the House of Lords.

The Tories gave way. They did not want to be outvoted in the House of Lords. The Reform Bill became law. And the Tories remained the biggest group in the House of Lords. They still are today.

E The House of Commons is shown in this painting of 1833.

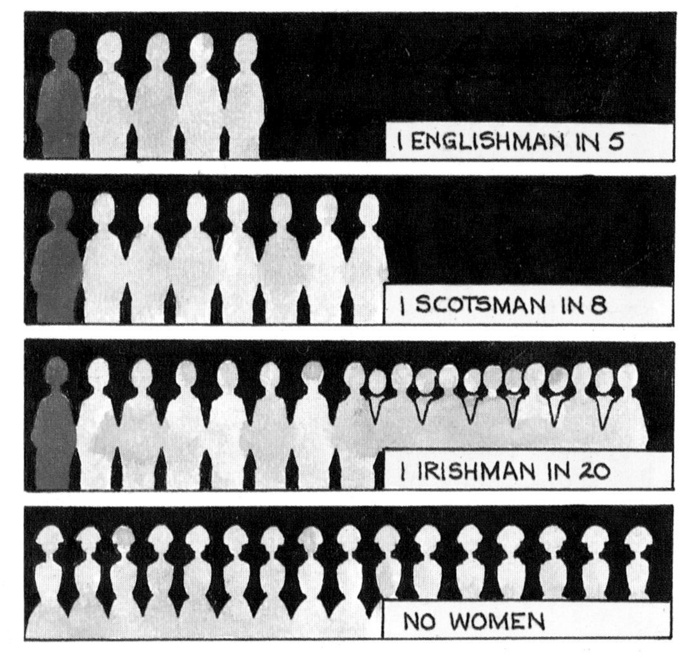

F Who got the vote after 1832.

G David Evans summed up the changes in *Wales in Modern Times* (1979).

For many, the Reform Act of 1832 was a great disappointment. There was no increase in the number of seats although some seats were [given] to the new industrial areas. The number of voters was increased but this still limited the right to vote to one-thirteenth of the population. The new voters were middle-class; the workers in both town and country gained nothing.

H Muriel Mansfield summed it up like this in *The House of History* (1931).

In 1832 the great Reform Bill became law, and the English people won a great victory for true progress in government. The country had made it clear that the will of the people must decide big questions; the story of the Reform Bill shows plainly that what the majority of the people want can always be gained through parliamentary government.

2 You need to watch a short video of a meeting of the House of Commons.
a) How are the scenes similar to source E?
b) List all the differences between these scenes.
c) Suggest reasons for these differences.

3 Study sources F, G and H.
a) Write down any opinions you can find in sources G and H. Explain why you think they are opinions and not facts.
b) Do you think sources G and H agree or not? Give reasons.
c) Why is it misleading to write that 'one-thirteenth of the population' got the vote?
d) Read this statement. 'The sources a historian uses will affect how he or she interprets events.' Explain in detail whether you agree, using the sources on these two pages.

CHARTISM

A This print shows a procession carrying the second Chartist petition (1842).

The Whigs and Tories were agreed on one thing: neither intended to give workers the vote. Yet the workers had been the ones out in the streets in 1831, throwing stones and rioting. Their violence had helped bring the Reform Act about.

There were more voters than before but they all now had to pay a fee to register. The House of Commons itself remained just as upper class after 1832 as it had been before.

For the workers, these were hard times. Some believed that trade unions might improve their lives. Others thought violence was the answer. A third group said there had to be more reforms of Parliament.

In 1838, representatives of various working groups met in Birmingham. They drew up a list of demands which would give the workers some control over Parliament. They called this list *The Charter*; this Charter gave the movement its name – *Chartism*.

The Chartists did not agree about how to persuade Parliament to give them what they wanted. Their main tactic was to draw up **petitions**. The first, in 1839, had over a million signatures. Parliament simply rejected it.

MPs did the same in 1842, when a second petition was presented. On each occasion, there was violence. Riots in Newport in 1839 were broken up by troops firing on the mob. A number of people died.

It was 1848 before the Chartists drew up yet another petition; it was to be their last. In April, they held a mass meeting on Kennington Common. They planned a procession to carry the monster petition to Parliament. But MPs, frightened of yet more riots, called in extra police and barred the way. The petition went by cab instead. A history textbook describes what happened next.

B *The House of History* by Dorothy Gordon (1932).

A great many signatures to the petition were afterwards found to be forged, so the whole movement became the subject of ridicule. About this time trade and wages began to improve, and the workers turned to other methods of bettering their conditions.

The six demands of the Chartists and the years in which they became law. Only one has not been granted.

C This is an early photograph, showing the Kennington Common meeting in 1848.

D This contemporary print shows the same scene. It was based on the photograph in source C.

E Part of a Chartist's speech. The speaker explains what the purpose of Chartism was.

The principle of the People's Charter means that every workman has a right to have a good hat and coat, a good roof, a good dinner, no more work than will keep him in health, and as much wages as will keep him in plenty.

F W E Adams: *Memoirs of a Social Atom* (1903). Mr Adams was a Chartist.

The first important business in which I was concerned was the National Petition for the Charter which was set afloat [in] 1848. It was alleged to have received 5,700,000 signatures; but the number was [later] reduced to 2,000,000, which included many **fictitious** names – the work of enemies in order to discredit the document. The [lively] scenes at our meetings where the petition lay for signature are still fresh in the memory.

One Chartist visitor was Mr Gammage, the author of a history of Chartism. Gammage's visit coincided with the General Election of 1852. We got him **nominated** so that he might make a speech. This was all we wanted, for it would have been utterly useless to go to the poll. Gammage made what we all thought was a capital speech for the Charter.

Accounts of the past may differ. One of the historian's tasks is to work out how and why they differ. School textbooks, for instance, always simplify history to fit the time available for history lessons.

1 Write down whether each source is primary or secondary and explain how you decided.

2 a) What were the demands in the Charter?
b) Be careful. Which of the six demands does source E mention?
c) Why did this person speak like this?
d) Look at source A. Which of the slogans shown was not one of the six demands?
e) What do sources A and E tell you about the *aims* of the Chartists?

3 a) Look at sources C and D. Write down the differences between them.
b) Read the captions. Suggest more than one reason why source D differs from source C.
c) Which source do you think is more useful for studying what happened? Give reasons.

4 a) Read sources B and F. How does source F add to your understanding of the petition?
b) Opponents of the Chartists claimed that the fake signatures were written by the Chartists themselves. Who do you think was right? Give reasons.
c) Is source B correct? Explain your answer.

PROTESTS FROM WOMEN

A This painting is called *Woman's Mission – Companion of Manhood* (1863).

The Whigs had introduced the 1832 Reform Act hoping that it would reform Parliament once and for all. They were wrong. In 1867, the Tories passed a Reform Act which gave the vote to every male householder in the boroughs. One in every three adult males now had the vote.

Yet women were still excluded. This was odd as Britain had been ruled by a woman (Queen Victoria) since 1837. Lord Chesterfield summed up the men's attitude: women, he said, were only big children. Some men thought that, if women had the vote, they would vote for whoever their father or husband told them to.

But times were changing. The number of well-off widows and unmarried women was increasing: many of them wanted the vote. They were supported by the Quakers, who had always treated men and women equally.

In 1867, Miss Lydia Becker founded the Manchester Women's Suffrage Committee. Regularly, she arranged for a bill giving women the vote to be introduced into Parliament. Each time, it failed.

The position of women was made more ridiculous when another Reform Act was passed in 1884. Over 2 million more men gained the vote, including farm labourers. Yet some of them were illiterate – they couldn't even read the ballot paper!

Most politicians did not want to give women the vote. Yet, as time passed, more and more men began to support the women's demands. In 1866, the writer John Stuart Mill had even sent a petition to Parliament, asking for women to be given the vote. It was no more successful than the Chartists' petitions had been.

There was one minor success. In 1869, some unmarried women were allowed to vote in local elections. Some women thought this was a poor reward for 50 years of peaceful campaigns. There had been riots before the 1832 Reform Act was passed. Was violence also needed to win women the vote? It was a tactic which 20th-century women would try.

B *The Outcast*, painted in 1851. A father tells his unmarried daughter to leave the house.

C This cartoon warned what would happen if women got the vote (1858).

D In 1871, Queen Victoria heard that Lady Amberley supported votes for women. She wrote:

The Queen is most anxious to enlist everyone who can speak or write to join in checking this mad, wicked folly of 'Women's Rights'. Lady Amberley ought to get a good *whipping*. Women would become the most disgusting of human beings if she were allowed to unsex herself. Where would be the protection which man was intended to give the weaker sex?

E Mrs Corbett, an authoress, wrote in the *Express* (1900).

Round about our docks, and scattered about the Marshes, are numbers of men who can't spell 'c-a-t, cat', much less a longer word. Their ignorance is only equalled by their [low way] of life. Their earnings are chiefly spent in public houses.

Yet anything in the shape of a man is privileged to vote. And anything in the shape of a woman is presumed to be unfit to do so. Brains and general usefulness don't count, that is clear.

F Winston Churchill wrote in 1895:

Only the most undesirable class of women are eager for this right. Those women who [do] their duty, [by] marrying and giving birth to children, are adequately represented by their husbands. Those who are unmarried can only claim a vote on the ground of property, which is [not] democratic

G New Zealand gave women the vote in 1893. Mrs Barncoat gave her views of this in 1900.

A serious argument against women's suffrage is the fact that in Wellington at last year's election two members (MPs) were elected who were as disreputable as [anyone] out of gaol in the place.

As it is quite certain that numbers of men would never have [voted for] them, numbers of women must have [done so]. The only possible explanation to me is that their wives and daughters may have gained them many women's votes – out of pity.

1 Draw a timeline for the years 1800-1900. On it, write all the events mentioned in this chapter.

2 a) Look at source C. Are the ladies supporting candidate 1 or 2? Explain how you decided.
b) Why are they supporting him? (Look carefully at the placards. There is more than one reason.)
c) Is the cartoonist in favour of votes for women? Explain how you decided.

3 a) What can you learn from sources A and B about attitudes to women at this time?
b) Read sources D to G. Which one(s) are in favour of votes for women? Give reasons.
c) Which one(s) are against? Again, give reasons.

4 All these sources come from Queen Victoria's reign. Which is most useful for understanding Victorian ideas about women? Explain fully how you decided.

REFORM FOR THE POOR

There were no government benefits in 1750 but the very poor could get help. A local tax called the poor rate was collected and shared out amongst those who needed assistance.

By the 19th century, this system had become very expensive indeed. In the middle of the 18th century, about £750,000 was raised; by 1818, it was nearly £8 million. People looked for ways of making savings.

In 1834, the government passed the Poor Law Amendment Act. Parishes would join together to form Unions and each Union would have a workhouse. The old and sick could still get help in their own homes but able-bodied poor people would have to go into the workhouse.

Inside, life was deliberately made as unpleasant as possible. For instance, married couples were forced to separate. The idea was to discourage people from seeking help. The theory was that people would rather find work than go into a workhouse.

This change was one of many which the government made after 1832. The government believed it was reforming the system: by 1837, the poor rates had dropped to £4 million. But the poor saw it differently. As one report from 1836 said, 'The workhouse is held in great dread.'

Yet workhouses survived into the 20th century. How did they change between 1834 and 1900? Study the sources on these two pages and draw your own conclusions.

A The rules at Southwell Workhouse, listed in the *Poor Law Commissioners Report*, 1834.

1 To separate males and females.
2 To prevent any visitors, and to make them keep regular hours.
3 To prevent smoking.
4 To disallow beer.
5 To find them work.
6 To treat and feed them well.

B A London workhouse in 1809.

DIETARY.

	BREAKFAST.	DINNER.	SUPPER.
Sunday	1 Pint of Oatmeal Porridge and ½ Pint of new Milk. (a)	½ pint of Broth 3½ oz. of Bread 8 oz. of Meat boiled ¾ lb. of Potatoes.	1 pint of Broth 7 oz. Bread
Monday	Ditto	1½ pint of boiled Barley or Rice with Milk and Treacle.	⅝ pint of new Milk 7 oz. Bread
Tuesday	Ditto	1½ pint of cold meat hash with Potatoes (b) 7 oz. Bread	Ditto
Wednesday	Ditto	14 oz. Suet Pudding and Treacle Sauce	Ditto
Thursday	Ditto	½ pint of Broth, 3½ oz. Bread, 8 oz. meat boiled ¾ lb. of Potatoes	1 pint of Broth 7 oz. Bread
Friday	Ditto	1½ pint Ox Head Soup either pea or vegetable 7 oz. Bread	⅝ pint of new Milk 7 oz. Bread
Saturday	Ditto	1½ pint of boiled Barley or Rice with Milk and Treacle.	Ditto

(a) Instead of this 1 pint of new milk and 7 oz. of bread, ~~may~~ to be given ~~where required at the discretion of the Master.~~ on Mondays. Wednesdays & Saturdays

(b) To be made up with fresh meat equal to a ½ lb. of meat per head, and to have in it equal to ¾ lb of potatoes per head.

Instead of Potatoes, Vegetables when in season.

Instead of one of the Barley or Rice Dinners, Fresh Fish and Potatoes may at the discretion of the visiting Guardians be substituted.

Such of the Inmates as are 60 years of ~~age or~~ upwards, may be allowed Tea or Coffee at Breakfast and Supper.

The Diet of the Sick to be according to the directions of the Medical Attendant.

5 oz. meat each meat day

no broth at dinner on a meat day

no treacle sauce

C The workhouse diet at Newcastle-on-Tyne (1837).

D George Lansbury described a visit to Poplar Workhouse, London, in 1892.

It was easy for me to understand why the poor dreaded and hated these places. These prison sort of surroundings were organized [to make] decent people endure any suffering rather than enter. Clothing was of the usual workhouse type, plenty of corduroy and blue cloth. No undergarments for either men or women, boots worn till they fell off. I inspected the supper of oatmeal porridge served up with pieces of black stuff floating around. We discovered it to be rat and mice manure.

E Charlie Chaplin described going into Lambeth Workhouse with his mother and brother in the 1890s. (From *My Autobiography*, 1964).

We were made to separate, Mother going in one direction, and we in another to the children's. How well I remember the sadness of that first visiting day! The shock of seeing Mother enter the visiting room [dressed] in workhouse clothes. How forlorn and embarrassed she looked! In one week she had aged and grown thin, but her face lit up when she saw us.

F T W Wilkinson visited a London workhouse in 1902. From *Living London* (1902).

What was the menu today, Tuesday? Roast mutton and potatoes, with bread. The young men and women each had four-and-a-half ounces of meat, twelve ounces of potatoes, and four ounces of bread. For breakfast the ration was four ounces of bread, one-pint-and-a-half of porridge or one pint of cocoa; and for supper it will be six ounces of bread and one-pint-and-a-half of broth.

... Now we reach the aged married couples' quarters – ten little rooms and a general room at the end for meals. Admirable is the only word for it. The brightly-painted walls, the pictures, the furniture, the photographs and knick-knacks belonging to the inmates, who are allowed to bring in such property and arrange it as they choose. If an old couple must spend their last days in the workhouse, one could wish them no brighter or more healthy quarters.

G A London workhouse, painted in 1878.

1 a) Describe the scene in source B.
b) Look at source G. Have conditions improved or not? Explain how you decided.

2 Please give reasons for your answers.
a) What was the attitude of people towards workhouses in the middle of the 19th century?
b) Had this changed by 1900?
c) Had food improved by 1902?
d) Had the rules changed by 1902?
e) Do you think the writers of sources D and F had the same opinion of workhouses? Give reasons.

3 a) Did the Poor Law Amendment Act bring progress? Explain your answer.
b) Do you think the Act was a reform or not? Please write a full and detailed answer.

9 US AND THEM: RELIGION

A A cartoon of a Church of England clergyman (1829).

Religion played a greater part in people's lives between 1750 and 1900 than it does today. The most powerful of the churches was the Church of England. The rich supported the Church of England – and the Church of England made it quite clear that it supported the rich. In many villages, the squire chose the vicar. In effect, the two of them ruled the village.

At Sunday services, the poor sat on benches towards the back; the rich sat in comfortable pews. Some even had their own boxes, with armchairs and a table. A servant might serve sherry during the sermon.

In the new industrial towns the Church of England had less impact. Most factory workers never went to church and many vicars did not even try to persuade them.

The Church was getting out of touch – and the people who decided to do something about it were the Methodists. The movement was started by John Wesley who had trained as an Anglican priest. He decided to travel the country to deliver his message.

Local priests kept him out of their churches so he preached in the open air instead. At first, the poor attacked him with stones and mud. By 1750, people were flocking to hear him speak. This 18th-century painting shows a Methodist meeting.

B

The Methodists preached in a way ordinary people could understand; they sang tuneful hymns with a simple message. It was that everyone was a sinner but Christ could save them all, both rich and poor. What they had to do was lead a Christian life – no swearing, drinking or gambling.

This did not make Wesley popular among the rich. They didn't like being told that they were as wicked as a factory worker. Nor did it please the Church of England: Anglicans disliked the fact that Methodists were working class.

So, in 1784, Wesley started the Methodist Church. It was run by the people themselves. A small group could meet anywhere and choose its own preacher. In many areas, the religions split on class lines. The well-off supported the Church of England; the poor attended the Methodist chapel. This happened in Wales. While the huge Anglican churches had empty seats, the chapels overflowed.

Sundays

C Sunday in 1850 (quoted in *Early Victorian England*, 1934).

When I was a young girl, we visited in the village, taught in the Sunday School and trained the choir. The servants wore bonnets on Sundays and went to church and sat in their own pew. There were boxed-in pews where the [rich] sat in state. The poor people waited to leave the church until the gentlefolk had made their way out. The men and women of the lesser order were separated, the men sitting on one side, the women on the other.

D Sunday in Hinckley, Leicestershire, in 1844. (Quoted by the *State of Towns Commission*.)

'How do people pass the Sunday?'

'[They] either spend their time exchanging fowls or bartering away their dogs, and so on, or in ranging the fields in the afternoon: after they have been lying a-bed, they take a stroll of three or four miles, come home weary and sleep away the afternoon.'

E Sunday in Edinburgh in the 1880s. (From *Edinburgh's Child* by Eleanor Sillar, 1961.)

There was no talk of making Sunday a happy day for a child – children had just to try to be happy through Sunday. I think our feeling about Sunday was that it was the waste of a perfectly good day.

It was certainly a day of bans and restrictions. The toy cupboard must not be opened, my dolls must lie abed. It was [a] sin to be seen with a needle in your hand. There must be no singing, except hymns.

F This cartoon showed a vicar travelling round his parish collecting tithes. The system dated back to the middle ages.

Historians disagree about the effects of Methodism. These are some of the views put forward.

Many sources are biased. In other words, they give a one-sided view of events or people. This is particularly true of cartoons. However, historians can still learn a great deal from biased sources.

1. a) Look at source F. What tithes has this vicar collected?
   b) How can you work out that this vicar is well-off? (There is more than one answer.)
   c) How do you think the cartoonist felt about this man? Give a reason.
2. a) Look at source A. What did this cartoonist think of clergymen? Please answer in detail.
   b) What can historians learn from this source? (More than one answer.)
   c) Would a photograph have been equally useful? Give a reason.
3. a) Read sources C, D and E. For each one, say whether it is about rich or poor people. In each case, give a reason. (Be careful.)
   b) Why would it be difficult to write about a 'typical' Victorian Sunday? (More than one answer.)
4. Which sources do you think help to explain why Methodism was popular among the poor? Explain your answer carefully.

RELIGION AND REFORM

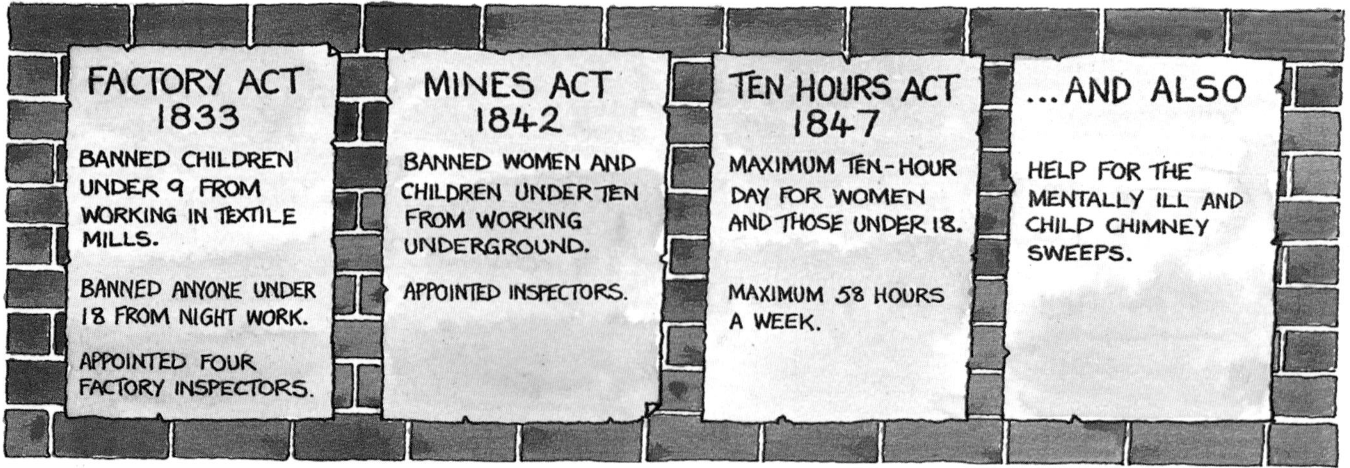

Some of the reforms which Lord Shaftesbury helped to bring about.

The Methodists had one other effect. Their success helped to stir the Church of England into new life. In the 19th century, many great reforms were the work of a number of very religious people.

One group was known as the Evangelicals. They thought that members of the Church of England ought to be doing more in the industrial towns; they believed that Christians should actually be *helping* the poor.

One of the best-known was Lord Shaftesbury, who gave much of his time and money to help the poor. On one occasion, he visited a school for the poor where the children were cold and hungry.

'What can we do for them?' he asked.

'God shall supply all their need,' the man in charge replied.

'Yes, he will,' agreed Shaftesbury, 'but they must have some food.' He immediately had two large churns of soup sent to the school.

It was not the only school Shaftesbury helped. There were no state schools in the early 19th century. For 39 years, Shaftesbury helped to run the Ragged Schools. These were free schools, paid for by charity.

Ragged school pupils were a mixed bunch. This analysis was made of the 2,345 pupils in the first 15 schools.

Many of the Evangelicals wanted to reduce working hours for children. They were concerned that the long hours left no time for religious education: the children were not growing up as Christians. One young miner, James Taylor, told officials in 1842 that he had 'never heard of Jesus Christ'. It was this sort of evidence which helped to convince the Evangelicals that children should be banned from mines.

Another group of Christians went even further. These were the Christian Socialists; they did not just try to help the poor. They wanted to change the system under which they lived. They wanted employers and workers to work together, instead of battling with each other.

The Christian Socialists helped workers to organise themselves in the early trades unions. They also helped to set up a Working Man's College in London, where working men could catch up on their education.

A Elizabeth Fry, a Quaker, founded an organisation to improve conditions for female prisoners in Newgate Gaol, London. This contemporary painting shows her reading to the prisoners.

Did the reforms bring progress?

B Norman Wymer wrote about the Mines Act in *Social Reformers* (1955).

By the end of July 1842 the coal-mining Bill was law, and thousands of women and children were freed from slavery.

C Angela V John discussed the results of the Act in *By the Sweat of Their Brow* (1984).

Prospects of finding [other] employment were severely limited. In Scotland there was some domestic service, seasonal field work and small textile mills which occasionally might have some work. By 1845 it was estimated that about 200 out of 4,200 Scottish colliery women had found work.

The intentions of [Shaftesbury] and his supporters were not that the women should replace [mining] with more pleasant employment. They [assumed] that the women should remain at home.

D Professor L Knowles commented on the results of the 1833 Factory Act in *The Industrial and Commercial Revolutions* (1921).

After the passing of the Factory Act there were grave difficulties. Of the 40,000 children thrown out of work, not one in a hundred was sent to school, as their parents were less able to pay school fees than before.

They tried to get the children [jobs] in factories not under the Act. If they could not do this the children ran wild about the streets. They often lost the benefit of the industrial training and got no other. Where they did get taken on in other factories this flood of children lowered the wages of those already working in them.

E Not all reformers were Evangelicals. Robert Owen set up this school for the children of workers at the New Lanark Mills – yet he was an atheist (1820s).

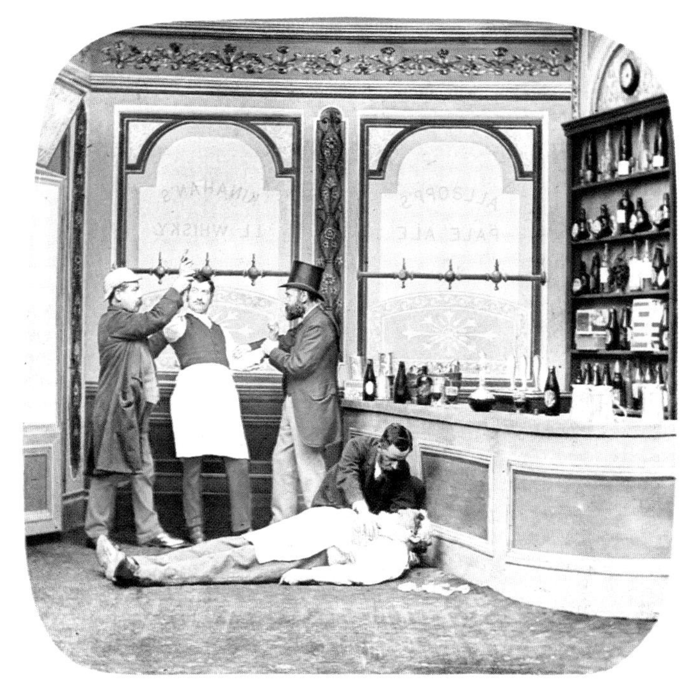

F The Methodists, in particular, tried to persuade people to give up alcohol. This slide stressed the effects of alcohol.

Secondary sources often disagree. No historian can study every primary source which is available. The result is that we have many interpretations of history. Each is affected by the sources used and the ways in which we use them.

1 a) Look at the pictures at the top of page 50. For the first three, write down why people thought this was a reform.
b) Read source D. What does it say were the results of the 1833 Act?
c) Does this mean that the Act was a failure? Explain your answer carefully.
d) Why would the Evangelicals have been disappointed to discover these effects?

2 a) Read sources B and C. What do you think Norman Wymer thought of the Act? Explain how you decided.
b) Do you think Angela John would agree? Explain how you decided.

3 a) You are a Scottish female miner, left without work after the 1842 Act. Write a letter to Lord Shaftesbury about your situation.
b) Exchange letters with a friend. Each write Lord Shaftesbury's reply to the woman.

4 'Lord Shaftesbury made great progress in helping working people.' Do you agree with this statement? Please give a detailed answer.

REFORM AND ANIMALS

A Bear baiting at Westminster (1821).

In 1750, few people would have said that the British were an animal-loving people. Indeed, foreigners often said how cruel they were. There was even a proverb: 'England is the hell of dumb animals'. Crowds gathered to watch cock and dog fights, rat killing and animals being baited.

Animal fights were seen as a special entertainment. Bull baiting was often laid on when a king or queen visited. While the dog tried to tear off the bull's skin, the bull tried to toss the dog into the air. Some men made a living by taking a bull round the country specially for such events.

Meanwhile, town streets were filled with horses and dogs pulling vehicles. Drivers used almost anything to get horses to go faster, including chains and shovels. In 1844, one driver lit a fire under his horse because it couldn't pull a heavy cart up a hill.

At Stamford, there was an annual festival when a bull was let loose in the town. Its body was smeared with soap and its nostrils filled with pepper. The inhabitants then tried to catch it.

In the middle of the 18th century, attitudes had begun to change. Poets wrote about the cruelty; newspapers published articles about it; books for children encouraged kindness towards animals.

Both Methodists and Evangelicals condemned cruelty. Many Christians believed that children who tortured animals grew into adults who murdered people. So, if people were kinder to animals, it might increase respect for law and order.

In the 19th century, governments passed laws to protect animals – and the RSPCA and its inspectors tried to make sure that laws were not broken. In 1887, Queen Victoria said that one of the changes which gave her real pleasure was 'the growth of more humane feelings towards the lower animals'.

Steps towards more humane treatment for animals.

B A social worker wrote in *The Reign of Queen Victoria* (1887).

Every class amuses itself more; amusements which were [once] thought to be the birthright of the upper classes alone are now shared by many. Prize-fighting, dog-fighting and cock-fighting have been condemned. Their places have been taken by sports and pastimes which are relatively free from brutality. The amusement that interests all classes most is still horse-racing; but cricket, football and other athletic sports have developed.

C Charles Walker described a regular event in Kelso, Scotland in *Strange Britain* (1989).

In the eighteenth century there was a cruel sport (fortunately now long-banned) in which a cat was placed in a barrel of soot, and the barrel suspended from a beam between two poles. Groups of 'whip-men' would then charge at the barrel on horseback and try to break it in with heavy blows from hammers and [sticks]. Eventually, the metal hoops would be dislodged and the cat would fall in a flurry of soot to the earth, where it was killed by [spectators].

D Bull baiting: a painting by Samuel Alken.

E Joseph Strutt commented on animal baiting in *The Sports and Pastimes of the People of England* (1801).

Bull and bear-baiting is not encouraged by persons of rank and [wealth] in the present day. It is attended only by the lowest and most despicable part of the people.

F Watching a cock fight at the Royal Cockpit, London.

1 a) Read source B. What is the writer's attitude towards animal fights? Explain how you know.
b) Read source C. What opinion does the writer express?

2 a) Read source E. What sort of people does he say attended baitings?
b) Look at sources A and D. Are the audiences the same as those described in source E? Explain your answer.
c) Suggest possible reasons for any differences.
d) Which of the following is more useful for understanding bull baiting: source D or paragraph 2 on page 52? Explain how you decided.

3 a) Study source A carefully. Write a paragraph describing this event from the point of view of an RSPCA inspector.
b) Write a paragraph describing the scene from the point of view of a spectator.

REFORM FOR SLAVES

The Evangelicals demanded many other kinds of reforms. One of them, William Wilberforce, worked hard to end slavery in the British Empire. Britain had been trading African slaves since the 16th century.

No one knows exactly how many Africans were sold as slaves in the Caribbean. Estimates vary between 10 and 15 million people. Possibly 25 per cent of them never finished the journey. Some jumped overboard and were eaten by sharks; others were killed by the crew. Yet more fell ill; they were thrown overboard alive to stop others from being infected.

Below deck, slaves were packed like sardines. They were chained together, hand and foot. Each sat in a space about 45 cms wide. From floor to ceiling, the maximum height was about 1.5 metres. No wonder that 'men strangled those next to them and women drove nails into each other's brains'.

Twice a day, they were led on deck to eat. They also had exercise – the crew, armed with whips, made them leap about the deck. Lighted matches were held to the ship's cannon, just in case there was a mutiny. Meanwhile, other sailors cleared up the vomit and excrement below deck.

Profits could be huge. Plantation owners paid up to five times what a slave cost in Africa. And it wasn't just the traders who benefited. Bristol grew rich on the slave trade. So did Liverpool. By 1800, 90 per cent of the European slave trade was run by Liverpool merchants. Local factories made the leg-irons and other equipment used in the trade.

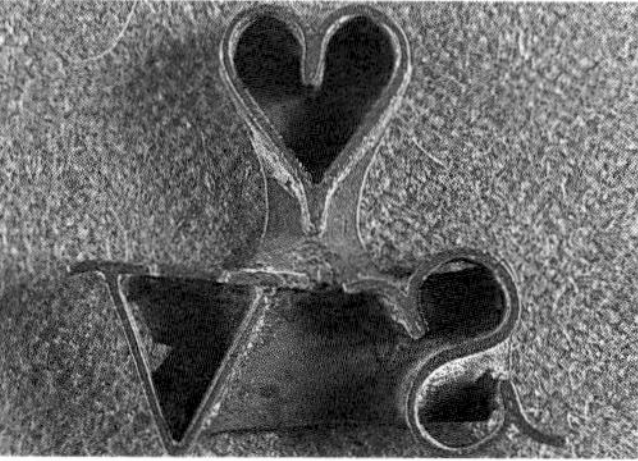

A A branding iron used in the Caribbean.

The merchants invested this wealth in factories and canals. Their capital helped James Watt to build his steam engine. They helped to pay for a railway line from Liverpool to London. In short, the slave trade helped to pay for Britain's industrial revolution.

It took Wilberforce and others over 40 years to end slavery in the British Empire. In 1807, Parliament made it illegal to buy or sell human beings. Those who were already slaves had to wait longer for their freedom: slavery itself was not abolished until 1833. 'Thank God,' said Wilberforce, 'that I have lived to witness this day.' He himself died just days later.

B An American slave market in 1840.

How was the trade organised?

C James Burke described how the slave trade worked in *The Day the Universe Changed* (1985).

The slave trade followed a regular pattern. Textiles and goods went to Africa to buy slaves which were transported to the West Indies, where they would work in the sugar plantations.

Sugar was brought back to Europe or taken to [America] to pay for tobacco which had a profitable market in Europe. Profits from this triangular trade were enormous.

D John Patrick and Mollie Packham wrote this in *Years of Change* (1989).

When the traders had sold the slaves, some picked up cargoes of sugar, rum or timber to take back to Britain, but most sailed back empty.

E John Rawley wrote about the triangular trade in *The Transatlantic Slave Trade* (1981).

A computer analysis of ship [voyages], 1715-65, found little evidence to support the myth of the triangular trade. Direct trade with one region was usual.

F Reformers used diagrams such as this to prove how bad conditions were on slave ships.

G James Boswell lived from 1740-95. He wrote this.

[It] would be cruel to the African savages [to abolish the slave trade]. It saves some of them from massacre, or **bondage** in their own country, and introduces them to a much happier state of life.

H This cartoon was produced by reformers. The man on the left is a slave owner.

I Many white people believed that they were a superior race. This was what one speaker said in 1866.

50,000,000 blacks have been placed on this magnificent globe of ours for [a] purpose. It is therefore our duty to [use] this large mass of human beings. [We must reject] at once the theory of equality. One section must govern the other.

Why did slavery end?

J The *Children's Encyclopaedia*, published in England in about 1950.

There were still slaves in British possessions up till the nineteenth century. At last, in 1759, a man was born who wiped the foul blot from our honour. He was William Wilberforce.

K A West Indian historian wrote this in *Capitalism and Slavery* (1944).

The **abolitionists'** importance has been greatly exaggerated. When British merchants depended on the West Indies they ignored slavery or defended it. When they found the West Indian sugar industry had become a nuisance, they destroyed slavery. What really counted were the forces of economic not moral change. The abolitionists [helped] the process along.

The sources on these two pages show some of the problems which historians face. For instance, sources C to E give different interpretations of the slave trade. With some of the pictures, you need to ask how reliable they are. Finally, you should find two sources which are biased – in other words, they give a very one-sided view of things.

1 a) What can you learn about slavery from (i) source A and (ii) source B?
b) Look at all the pictures. Which ones do you think are reliable? Give reasons.
c) Which ones do you think might be unreliable? Explain why they might not be reliable.
d) What other sources would you want to use to check the sources you chose for question (c)? Explain how you decided.

2 a) How do sources C and D disagree?
b) How do sources C and E disagree?
c) Which of these three sources do you trust and why?
d) Are sources G and I giving facts or opinions? Answer carefully.
e) What can a historian learn from sources G and I?

3 a) Read sources J and K. How do they disagree?
b) Suggest a reason why they disagree. Please answer in detail.

10 TRADE IN THE 19TH CENTURY

1750 1775 1800 1825 1850 1875 1900

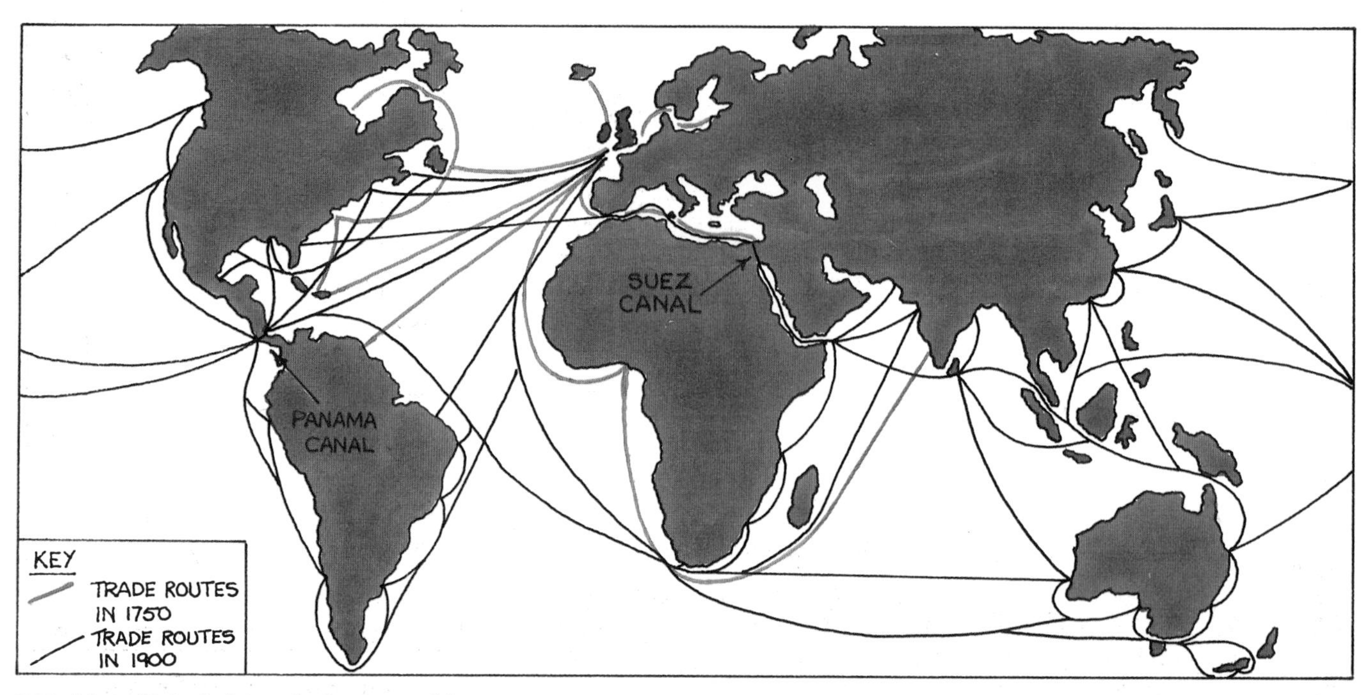

A How Britain's trade increased between 1750 and 1900.

Britain was the first country to have an industrial revolution. It meant that goods could be produced faster and more cheaply in Britain than anywhere else on earth. Britain led the way in industries such as coal, cotton, iron and steel, and shipbuilding.

By 1850, Britain produced half of the world's manufactured goods; Britain had one-quarter of the world's trade. No wonder people described Britain as the 'workshop of the world'.

By then, it suited Britain to have a policy of 'free trade'. In other words, the government did not tax imports of food or raw materials. And it encouraged manufacturers to sell goods abroad. The diagram opposite explains why.

There was no real risk in this policy. Britain had the biggest empire in the world and a powerful navy to control its trade routes. In fact, it was in Britain's interests for new countries to be opened up. Imports of Australian wool helped to clothe the growing British population. Canadian corn helped to feed it.

When steamships replaced sailing ships, faster transport was possible. Canada could send live cattle across the Atlantic Ocean. When refrigeration was invented, South America sent frozen meat and butter. So did New Zealand.

A country must trade with others to keep up its standard of living. Source D shows how successful Britain's trade was. Demand for British exports meant that there were usually plenty of jobs available. Most workers in 1900 were better fed and clothed than their ancestors of 1750.

As trade increased, so firms grew larger. New machinery was a big investment which one owner might not be able to afford. The solution was to ask people to invest money in the business by buying shares. If the firm was successful, these shareholders shared the profits in the form of dividends. This is how most large businesses are run today.

HOW FREE TRADE BENEFITED BRITAIN

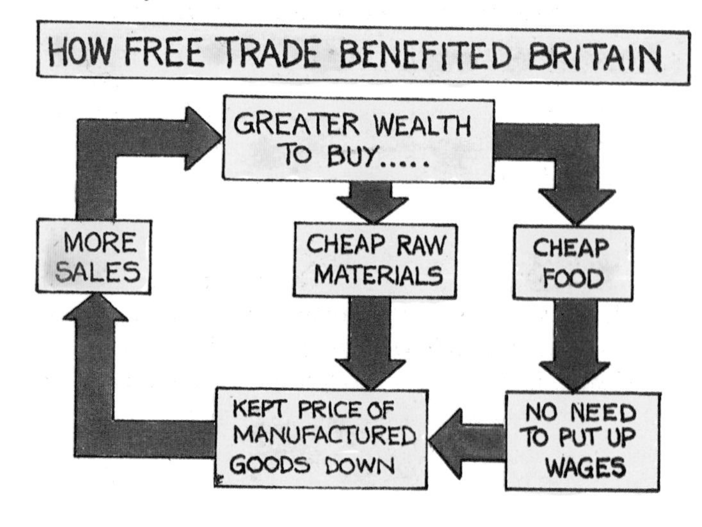

B The port of Liverpool in about 1750.

C The port of Liverpool in 1907.

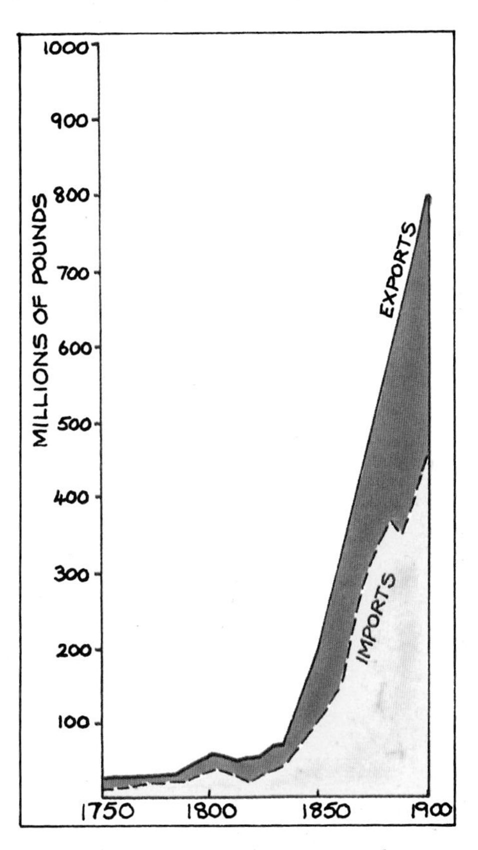

D How the value of Britain's exports and imports grew between 1750 and 1900.

E From William Cobbett's *Northern Tour* (1832).

All the way along, from Leeds to Sheffield, it is coal and iron, and iron and coal. It was dark before we reached Sheffield; so that we saw the iron furnaces in all [their] horrible splendour . . .

It is impossible to behold it without being convinced that, whatever other nations may do with cotton and wool, they will never equal England [for] things made of iron and steel. This Sheffield is one bed of iron and coal. They call it black Sheffield, and black enough it is; but from this town and [the nearby area] go nine-tenths of the knives that are used in the whole world.

Trade made Britain rich in the 19th century. There was, of course, more than one reason why Britain's trade was doing so well. Historians first try to discover the causes, then they try to decide which cause was most important.

1 a) Look at sources B and C. How has the scene changed between 1750 and 1907?
b) What, if anything, remained the same?

2 a) Look at source A and use a modern atlas. Which new countries was Britain trading with by 1900?
b) Study source D carefully. How does this prove that Britain's trade was successful?

3 a) Read the text on page 56. Write down the reasons why Britain grew rich in the 19th century. You should find *at least* three.
b) Look at your list. Which of the causes do you think was most important? Explain how you decided.
c) Britain was called 'the workshop of the world'. What do you think this means?
d) How does source E support this view?

4 How did the following benefit from Britain's successful trade: (a) factory-owners, (b) workers and (c) the country itself? In each case, write down as many ways as possible.

11 THE EMPIRE GROWS

1750 1775 1800 1825 1850 1875 1900

A This German slide of 1900 was entitled 'The Human Races'. Europeans thought that they were the superior race.

By 1900, Britain had gained an empire bigger than any empire the world had ever known. A quarter of the world's population was ruled by the government in London. Maps of the time showed great areas in red: it meant they were British.

In 1750, it had been very different. The American colonies and the West Indies made up most of the empire. In 1775-83, the Americans fought the British and won their freedom. Overnight, much of the empire was lost.

This loss led to a change of attitude back in Britain. For nearly 100 years, many people thought that colonies were a waste of time. It cost money to defend them. 'Why waste it?' some people asked: sooner or later a colony would want to be free.

By 1870, attitudes had changed yet again. As a result, from 1870 onwards, there was a great scramble for colonies. It wasn't just Britain that wanted a great empire. So did most other European countries. What had happened? How did Britain build up such a huge empire?

First, there were economic reasons. Years earlier, merchants had staked out claims in Africa and India. The trading posts they built grew into whole areas controlled by Britain. Britain needed these markets to sell her manufactured goods. Colonies had the added advantage that they produced cheap food and raw materials as well.

New technology also played a part. The new steamships needed coal; ports, such as Aden, were established where they could refuel on long journeys. In time, these coaling stations grew into colonies. But steamships also meant that the colonies could be reached more quickly. So troops could be rushed out to put down any revolt.

B Colonies were useful for getting rid of unwanted criminals. Australia was used in this way from 1788 to 1867, when the last convicts were transported. This picture shows convicts going aboard a prison-ship.

Steamships meant the colonies were easier to get to; railways meant they were easier to get across. The first settlements were just on the coast. But railway tracks could be laid right through a colony. Whole new markets opened up for traders.

In turn, steamships and railways created the demand for yet more raw materials; industry boomed. The demand for manufactured goods rose higher and higher.

Gold was discovered in Australia in 1851 and diamonds in South Africa in 1867. By 1900, millions of Britons had set sail in search of their fortune; many never returned.

Competition was another cause. As long as Britain controlled a colony, it meant that other countries could not. In the 1880s, new British trading companies laid claim to huge areas of the African continent.

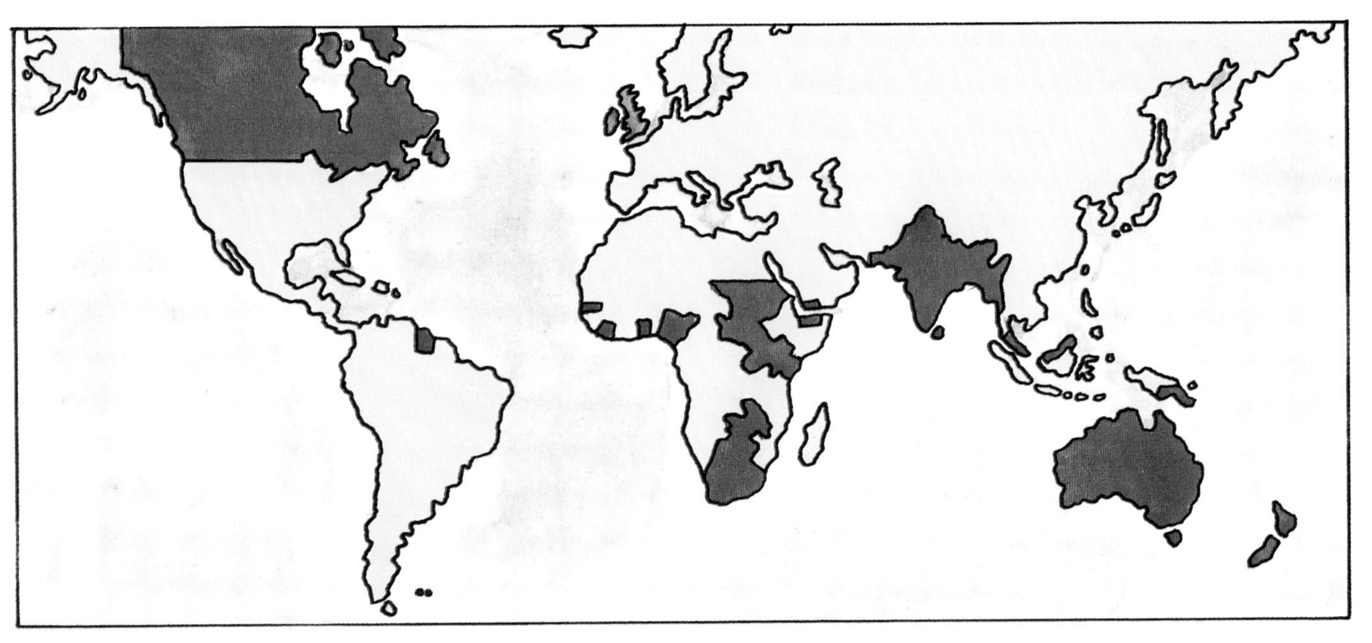

C The British Empire in 1900. Excluding India, its population grew from 4 million (1837) to over 50 million (1900).

Once there, colonists knew the British government would send help, if they needed it. When fighting broke out on their boundaries, the troops would arrive – and, very often, a new area of land would be taken over to ensure peace in future.

Amongst all the merchants and adventurers, a few individuals played a key part. Cecil Rhodes, for instance, wanted to see the map of Africa coloured red. He felt it was the best thing that could happen to the African people. The British, he said, were 'the best people in the world. The more of the world we inhabit, the better it is for humanity.'

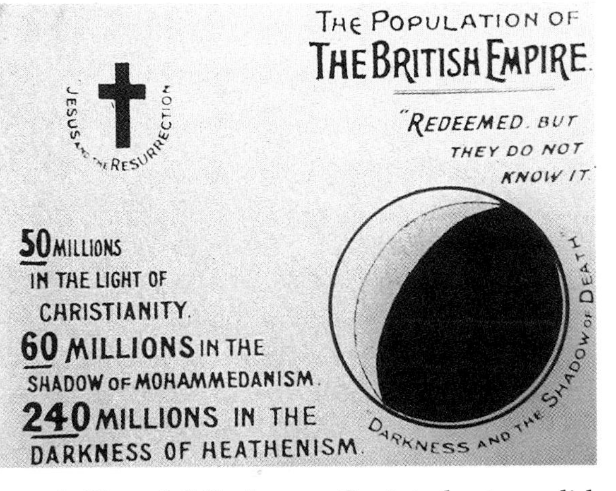

D A Church Missionary Society lantern slide from the 1890s. The Church believed its duty was to convert heathens. (The '60 millions' were Muslims.)

E A comic slide used in Methodist Sunday Schools in the 1880s.

1 a) What can you learn from sources D and E about attitudes towards the empire?
b) Why do you think Christians held the views shown in these slides?
c) Would Cecil Rhodes have approved of the slides? Explain your view.

2 This question is about causes.
a) Divide your page into five sections, each headed with one of these words: economic; technological; cultural; military; religious.
b) Now, read these two pages to discover what caused Britain to gain her empire. Write down each cause you find in the correct section.
c) What links can you find between the economic and technological causes? Please answer in detail.

THE BRITISH AND THEIR EMPIRE

WANTED, EMIGRANTS FOR CANADA.—Farmers, Labourers, Servant Girls, &c.—For free pamphlets apply Passenger Department, Canadian Pacific Ry., 67 and 68, King William-street, E.C., or 30, Cockspur-street, S.W.
Agency of Allan, American, Cunard, Dominion, Norddeutscher, White Star, &c.

A Advertisement from the *Evening News* (1900). By then, many families had relatives in the colonies.

Britain's colonies helped make the nation rich. But, more than that, the Empire affected the lives of everyone in many little ways. For instance, mutton pies became a popular working-class treat in the late 19th century: much of the mutton was imported from Australia.

For the middle classes, the Empire offered a career: huge numbers of government officials were needed to rule the colonies; engineers were needed to build railways and public buildings; merchants set off to organise trade.

The rich had other uses for the Empire. It provided a way of getting rid of the surplus population. Scottish and Irish landowners paid for people to emigrate. The government, too, encouraged people to settle in the colonies: cheap fares to Australia were offered in the 1830s.

In the 18th century, relatives might never have heard from the emigrants again. But cheap postage in the later 19th century meant they no longer needed to lose touch. Ordinary working people learned from relatives' letters about the great British Empire 'on which the sun never set'.

B Advertisers saw the value of Empire. The figure of Britannia was used to sell all sorts of products.

While millions of Britons were leaving for the colonies, people from the colonies were emigrating to Britain. There were about 20,000 black people living in Britain in 1750. When the slave trade ended, many went home. But others kept arriving.

London had more immigrants than most towns. On London's streets in 1850 more than half the pamphlet sellers were either black or Asian. Others carried advertising boards, as in this contemporary painting.

Yet the working class took little interest in their empire for most of the 19th century. But, as the empire grew, so did British pride in it.

This new interest was partly caused by compulsory education after 1880. And the new popular daily newspapers helped to stir up enthusiasm. The government also encouraged it. 'England without an empire!' the Colonial Secretary once exclaimed. 'Can you conceive it?'

D Cardiff was one of the ports which grew rich in the 19th century. This fireplace in the castle shows people's pride in their city.

E The Records of the New Zealand Company listed those people applying to emigrate. These are a few of them.

George Wain and wife
Are both healthy and respectable.
William Barker
Of good character, an excellent general workman – understands smith's work in general, also shoeing and tin work. Is robust and healthy.
Francis Doughty
Single, pretended blacksmith – unfit for a colony – very dirty and very poor and illiterate.
Sarah Ann Webb
Is very respectable in appearance and manner – is robust and healthy; has promised to join her brother who is gone out on the *Cuba*. The remainder of the family will follow next year if accounts are favourable.
William Horton, wife and family
Is given to drinking and unable to pay the children's passage.
William Welch and wife with 7 children
A strong healthy couple. Have an excellent character from their late employer. Welch has such a perfect knowledge of all kinds of out-of-door labour that I consider him one of the best of his class I have yet met with. He will pay for the 6 children under age.

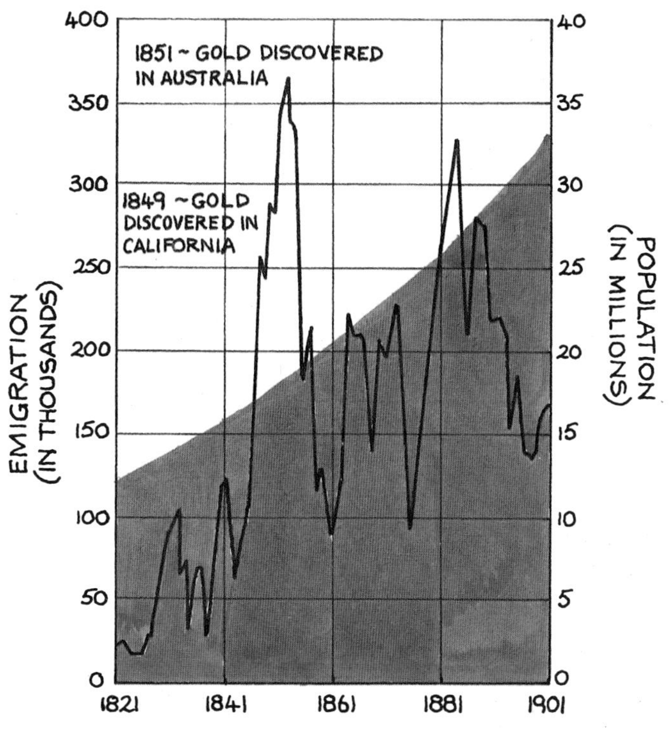

F Britain's population and emigration figures, 1821-1901.

Every source is useful but not necessarily for a particular enquiry. So a historian studies every source carefully to see what can be learned from it. When studying why people emigrated, one source may be more useful than others.

1. a) What can you learn from sources A and E about why people emigrated?
   b) Which is more useful for explaining why people generally emigrated? Give reasons.
2. Give reasons for your answers.
   a) Which source is most useful for understanding why the colonies needed people?
   b) For what sort of enquiry would source C be useful?
3. These two pages include examples of ways in which the British used their empire.
   a) Write down all you can find.
   b) For each one, explain how it benefited (i) Britain and (ii) the colony.
   c) Do you think the development of the empire is an example of progress or not? Explain your answer carefully.
4. Read source E. Which of these people would you have allowed to enter New Zealand? Explain why you chose or rejected each of them.

12 IRELAND

Historians study what caused events in the past. By now, you should know that an event usually has many causes and you will realise that some causes are more important than others. These causes are often linked. In other words, one cause can itself cause other causes – and so on.

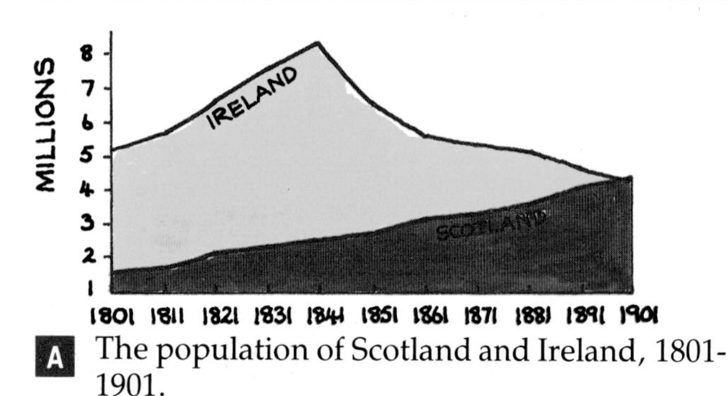

A The population of Scotland and Ireland, 1801-1901.

If you look at the graph above, you will notice something odd. While the population of Scotland was going up, the population of Ireland was falling. When did the Irish population start falling and what could have caused it? Perhaps it might be quickest if we consult a textbook.

B This is how Dorothy Gordon explained it in *The House of History* (1932).

In 1845 potato disease ruined the crop in Ireland, which meant starvation for the Irish peasants.

That seems clear enough. The potato crop suffered a disease and the Irish peasants starved to death. It happened in 1845, which explains why there was a drop in the population between 1841 and 1851. But is this the whole story?

1 a) Look carefully at the graph. What does source B fail to explain?
b) How would a historian set about explaining it?

Source B is, of course, by no means the whole story. There was nothing new about a potato shortage. Indeed, hunger was a part of an Irish peasant's life. In 1820, the Duke of Wellington had written that starvation happened every year in Ireland. And this was not the first time that the potato crop had failed.

You will find various sources on the remainder of these two pages; they will help to explain what happened in Ireland in the 1840s and why it had such serious effects. Please bear in mind that it is not possible to include everything in this space.

C Revd Sydney Smith wrote in the *Edinburgh Review* (1820).

Seven or eight months out of twelve, in many parts of Ireland, there is no constant employment of the poor; and the potato farm is all that shelters them from famine. There is little manufacture. The price of labour is low, the demand for labour irregular.

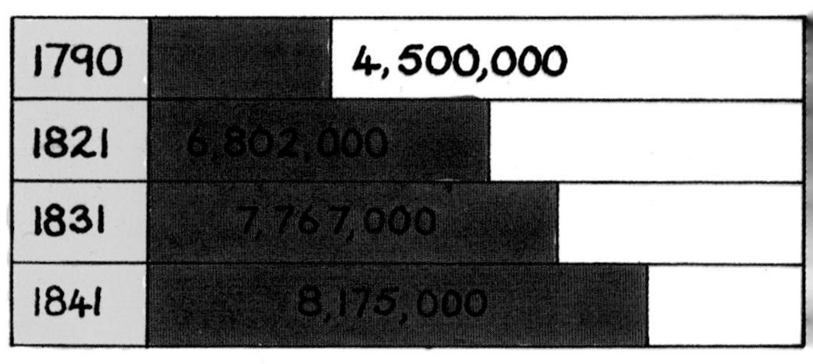

Year	Population
1790	4,500,000
1821	6,802,000
1831	7,767,000
1841	8,175,000

D Despite this, the population of Ireland was rising, as these figures show.

With very few jobs in industry, most Irish had to earn a living by farming. That meant that everyone wanted their own plot of land. As the population grew, so did the demand for land. As a result, the plots grew smaller. Tenants split up their land so that each of their sons would have his own plot. Nearly half of these plots were two hectares or less.

The introduction of steamships had increased the export of food from eastern Ireland to England.

E *The Evicted*: a 19th-century painting.

F Much of the land was owned by English people who did not live in Ireland. W Steuart-Trench was an agent for one of these landowners. (From *Realities of Irish Life*, 1868.)

The estate had been neglected. Nothing had been done to stop the subdivision of land. Boys and girls married at the age of seventeen or eighteen, without thinking it necessary to have anything [except] a shed to live in, and a small plot of land to grow potatoes.

By now, you might be wondering why the Irish didn't grow corn instead. If the potato crop had failed before, wouldn't it have been sensible to grow something else?

G C Woodham Smith explained why the Irish grew potatoes in *The Reason Why* (1953).

Potatoes need only one third of the [land that] wheat [needs], grow anywhere, can be stored in the ground and shared with fowls and pigs. The Irish came to live on the largest, coarsest, most heavy cropping kind known. They ate this potato boiled, and they ate nothing else. Over great [areas] of Ireland any form of cooking [except] boiling a potato in a pot became unknown.

There were other reasons why the Irish relied on the potato. It is one crop which will grow well even on poor land – and much of the land *was* poor. Not only that, but a hectare of potatoes provided more food than any other crop. But even that had disadvantages, as Reverend Smith explained.

H Revd Sydney Smith: *Edinburgh Review* (1820).

It is so easy to rear a family upon [potatoes] that . . . the population goes on [rising]. They have increased the population so fast and kept the price of labour so low that the Irish poor have never been able to emerge from their mud cabins. Many more live [because] of the introduction of potatoes, but all live in greater wretchedness.

I An Irish peasant's house in the 19th century.

2 a) Why did a potato disease cause Irish peasants to starve to death? List as many causes as you can.
b) Which of these causes were long-term causes? Explain how you decided.
c) Which of the causes do you think were most important? Explain how you decided.
d) Who might have prevented the Irish from starving to death? Give reasons for your answer.

3 a) Write your own detailed account of why there was famine in Ireland in 1845.
b) Compare your version with source B. Which is a better explanation? Give reasons.

FAMINE AND AFTERWARDS

The potato harvest of 1845 was disastrous. A mystery fungus attacked the potato crop and destroyed it. Stinking plants rotted in the fields. Potatoes are harvested in the autumn, so the summer of 1846 brought famine.

That year, the Irish sowed plenty of potatoes and hoped for a better crop. It failed yet again. By 1847, they no longer had the reserves to sow for a big crop; as it happened, it was a good crop but much too small. The years 1848 and 1849 brought more failure.

One result was inevitable. About a million people either starved to death or died of fever. There was similar suffering in the Scottish Highlands where people also depended on potatoes. People ate dandelion roots and nettles or even the bark from trees.

A Old Chapel Lane, Skibbereen, in 1846. (See source C.)

The government took action to reduce the price of corn but the Irish peasants just could not afford it. In any case, Irish peasants rarely saw money. They paid their rent by working for the landlord or by giving him goods – just as peasants had in the middle ages.

The bad harvests meant that the peasants could not pay their rent. The landlords' solution was to evict them. Source H is a photograph from later in the century but the process had not changed.

By 1851, Ireland's population had dropped by over 1.6 million. At first, starvation and fever were the main causes. But from 1848 onwards, many of the Irish took matters into their own hands. Rather than die, they emigrated.

B *The Emigrants Departure*, painted in 1864.

Many sailed for the United States, bitter about how they had been treated. They collected money for a group called the Fenians who attacked the British police and army in the 1860s. The English called them criminals; the Irish called them patriots .

Others came to Britain to find work. There was nothing new in this. In the 1830s, about 250,000 Irish immigrants came to England and Wales each year. There was very little manufacture in Ireland because the British government did not want competition. In any case, Ireland lacked both iron and coal.

Liverpool was a favourite destination because it was easy to reach from Ireland. Few of the newcomers had ever learned a trade. The only tool which most had used was a potato-spade.

As a result, they mostly did unskilled jobs. In general, the Irish took the jobs which the English did not want – and that included serving in the army and navy. Few went back home to live. Even today, the population of Ireland is less than half what it was in 1841.

C Mr Cummins saw the suffering in Skibbereen in Cork. He described it in a letter.

In the first [house] six famished and ghastly skeletons were huddled in a corner on some filthy straw. Their sole covering [was] what seemed a ragged horse-cloth. Their wretched legs [hung] about, naked above the knees. I found, by a low moaning, they were alive. The same morning, the police opened a house on the lands [nearby], and two frozen corpses were found lying upon the mud floor.

D The 1851 census reported:

Generally speaking, the starving people lived upon the carcases of diseased cattle, upon dogs and dead horses, but [mainly] upon the herbs of the field, nettle tops, wild mustard and water cresses. Even in some places dead bodies were found with grass in their mouths.

E Irish vagrants in England: a painting of 1853-4.

F Some immigrants became street-sellers. The number of Irish street-sellers in London doubled during the 1840s. Henry Mayhew interviewed one young woman in London (1851).

It's a poor livin' when I see how others live. Yes, in thruth, sir, but it's thankful I am for to be able to live at all, at all. [My parents] was evicted. The family of us was. The thatch of the bit o' home was tuk off above our hids, and we were lift to the wide worruld.

It was Bristol we come to. We walked all the long way to London. My parints died of the cholera, and I live with mysilf. I don't make [3p] a day. I may make [2½p]. There's a good many young papple I know is now sillin' in the streets becase they was evicted in their own counthry. I suppose they had no where ilse to come to. I'm niver out of a night.

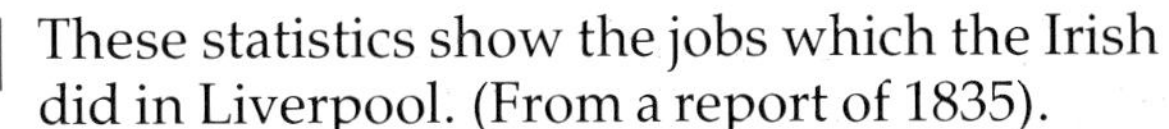

G These statistics show the jobs which the Irish did in Liverpool. (From a report of 1835).

Job	Number
Mechanics	780
Brickworkers	270
Sugar boilers	200
Masons' labourers	350
Bricklayers' labourers	850
Chemical works and soaperies	600
Sawyers	80
Loading in the docks	1,700
Porters in warehouses	1,900
Coal heavers and sundry	430
Other labourers	340

H A photograph of an evicted family.

Consequences, like causes, may be short term or long term.

1. This question is about consequences.
   a) What were the results of the famine for the Irish peasants?
   b) What were the results of the famine for Ireland?
   c) Which of these results were long term? Explain how you decided.
2. a) Look at source H. What has been done to this house by the landlord?
   b) Why has this been done?
   c) Was the family well-off or poor? Explain how you decided.
3. a) Look at source B. Roughly how old do you think the young woman is?
   b) Why could Ireland not afford to lose people of this age?
   c) What thoughts might be going through the young woman's mind?
   d) Read source F. Do you think this young woman's hopes were fulfilled? Explain your answer.

13 PHOTOGRAPHS AS SOURCES

1750 1775 1800 1825 1850 1875 1900

When the first cameras appeared in the 1840s, people predicted that painting was dead. Who would want a painting when an accurate photo could be taken instead? After all, 'the camera cannot lie', can it?

If that is true, then photographs should be some of our best sources for learning about Victorian Britain. Unfortunately, it is not as easy as that. These cameras needed an exposure time of some minutes. In other words, if you were photographing people, they had to stand still for that long. As a result, pictures of people had to be posed.

Indoors, it was even more difficult, even with the best lighting. The photographer used head clamps and arm props to help the unfortunate sitter to stay still. This photograph of Princess Alexandra, wife of the future King Edward VII, shows her propped up by an 'iron maiden'. No wonder that the people always looked so formal.

A

Until the 1860s, few photos showed totally natural scenes. Photographers thought of themselves as artists. They composed a scene, just as a painter would.

The first small hand cameras appeared in the 1860s. By the 1870s, it was possible to take a picture in less than a second. Of course, this did not stop photographs being posed. This picture was taken in 1895.

B

Some of the best photographers of the time produced photographs for magic lantern shows. But the historian must treat even these rather carefully. Lantern shows were put on to entertain people. Well-off people were fascinated by pictures of slum life. This one dates from the 1890s.

C

D Paul Martin was one of the first photographers to take snapshots, as we do today. He took this photograph at Yarmouth in 1892.

E A painter's view of the seaside. William Frith painted *Life at the Seaside* after a visit to Ramsgate in 1851.

Historians must assess photographs just as they would assess any other source. The camera may not lie but the photographer may have distorted reality in some way, perhaps by making people pose. Despite this, we can learn a great deal from Victorian photographs about how people lived in the 19th century.

1 a) What are the differences between D and E?
b) What is similar in the two pictures?
c) Which is more useful for a historian? Give reasons.

2 a) What can you learn from source D that you cannot learn from source E?
b) What questions do you need to ask about a photograph before relying on it as evidence? Please answer in detail.
c) Think carefully. How useful are sources B and C to a historian? Please answer in detail.

14 A LAST LOOK AT WORKERS

1750 1775 1800 1825 1850 1875 1900

Changes in laws affecting working conditions.

The government went on reforming working conditions during the second half of the 19th century. Some of the changes are shown above. The government had also tightened up on coal mines. In 1860, for instance, boys under 12 were not allowed below ground unless they could read and write.

But it was impossible to check every small workshop; nor could inspectors see what went on at home. So there was no way of stopping young children from working. The solution was to make education compulsory. By 1900, all children aged up to 12 had to attend school.

One other change was happening. Holidays had been strictly for the rich in 1750. Employers did not give paid holidays and poor people could not afford to take time off work. Even weekends were short: most people worked right through Saturday.

The Factory Act of 1850 began to change this. It stopped women and young people from working after 2pm on Saturday. There was little point in keeping machines going when these workers had left. So most factories sent the men home as well. However, this only applied to factories – and only 50 per cent of industrial workers worked in factories.

In 1871 another law was passed which still affects all workers today. The government decided which days should be bank holidays. At last, most British workers were guaranteed holidays, although they varied between countries.

But even bank holidays did not help one group of workers. These were the workers who worked on piece-rates. In other words, they got paid for the amount they produced. Often, they worked at home for very low pay. No laws had made their situation better, as the sources show.

A Girl workers at Coat's of Paisley in the late 19th century.

B A cartoonist's view of the dressmaking industry.

C Wages earned by women doing sprigging (embroidery) in Donegal, Ireland (1907).

We found that 5p was considered to be a good day's wage; and we were informed that the usual wage was 3.5p a day. Many old women can earn only [up] to 2.5p a day.

It was difficult to estimate the number of hours worked. Many of the women and girls had their duties in connection with the farm.

It seemed almost impossible for them to tell us the actual number of hours spent in sprigging.

[These were their wages:]

Handkerchiefs	3p a dozen	(1 dozen per day)
Handkerchiefs	6.5p each	(1 in 2 days)
Muslin tray cloth	4p	(2 days)
Muslin bedspread	20p	(nearly 1 week)
Tablecloth	15p	(4 days)
Ladies' skirts	25p each	(9 days)

D From *Living London* (1902).

Mrs P__________ is a widow who has for many years earned her living by making hat boxes at home. 'I have to [buy] the paste, and the needle and thread, and when I've finished a gross I get [12.5p]. I don't grumble at the pay, for when I can get the work I'm able to make a very decent living for a poor widow. It's only when we're slack I don't like it, for then I have to go out charing, and such work is a little beyond my strength.'

E Examples of weekly rates of pay in 1900.

Mule-spinner in a factory £2.00
Weaver in a factory £1.25
14-year-olds in textile factories 15p-60p
Lady's maid 50p-80p
Kitchen maid 30p-50p
Laundry maid 20p-40p

__1__ a) Draw a timeline for the years 1800-1900. Allow 1 cm for each decade. Mark on it laws which the government passed to reform industry. (Look back at pages 19 and 50-51.)
b) Who do you think benefited most from the changes – men, women or children? Explain how you decided.

__2__ a) Look at source B. What is happening at the numbered places?
b) What is the cartoonist's attitude towards the people you can see? Explain how you decided.

__3__ a) Which of these sources is most useful for learning about workers' standards of living? Give reasons.
b) Which of these sources is most useful for learning about working conditions? Again, give reasons.

__4__ 'Working conditions had improved greatly by 1900.' Do you agree or disagree with this statement? Use the sources to help you with your answer.

TRADES UNIONS

A Membership card of the Amalgamated Society of Engineers (1895).

The government helped workers by passing laws; other organisations tried to help workers, too. In the 18th century, skilled workers often combined together and paid money into a fund. It was a kind of insurance in case they fell ill.

In time, this idea developed into trades unions but it was not easy for workers. The government banned 'combinations' from 1799 to 1824, although workers often went on meeting in secret. The first big union was the Grand National Consolidated Trades Union (GNCTU) of 1834. It claimed to have half a million members but it soon collapsed.

Skilled workers, such as spinners, had not joined the GNCTU. They were busy building up small local clubs into the great national unions we have today. The first of these, for engineers, appeared in 1851.

The Amalgamated Society of Engineers had paid officials to run union affairs. Within ten years, they had built up funds of £73,000. They did not waste these on strikes, if they could avoid it. The union soon became a force to be reckoned with.

Other skilled workers, like the carpenters, soon followed their lead. The first union just for women was founded in 1872. Its members were sempstresses in Edinburgh.

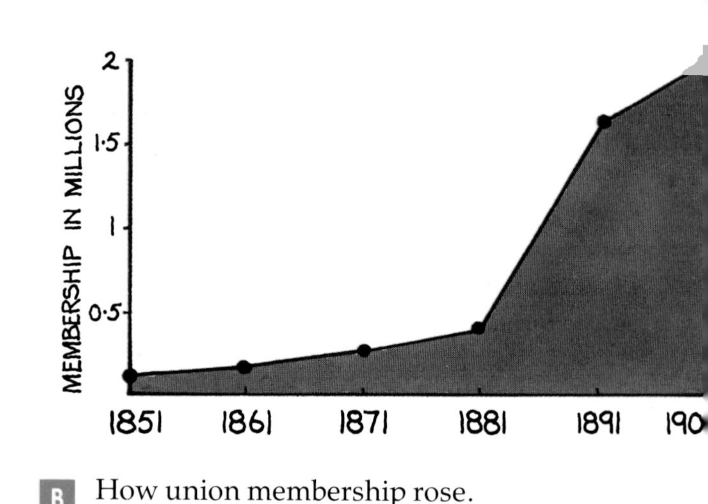

B How union membership rose.

The unskilled workers were some of the last to form unions. The first successful strike by unskilled workers was at Bryant and May's match factories in London. About 1,400 girls went on strike to get better conditions and improve their weekly pay of just 20p.

Their success was followed in 1889 when the London gas workers were promised an eight-hour day. That same year, the London dockers demanded a minimum wage of 2.5p an hour. They, too, were successful.

Yet workers still felt that the main political parties did not represent them. Some of their leaders thought the solution was to stand for Parliament. One of them was a Scottish miners' leader, Keir Hardie. In 1892, he became one of the first working-class MPs. In the following year, he helped start a new workers' party – the Independent Labour Party.

C This union banner shows Keir Hardie (top left) in old age.

D This trade union banner dates from the 1890s.

E A modern historian, C P Hill, described the dockers' strike in *British Social and Economic History* (1957).

In the summer of 1889 the London dockers struck for a minimum wage of [2.5p] an hour. It was a good time to come out – a warm summer, and trade was booming. For nearly four weeks the port of London was closed. The middle class of London came to [sympathise] with the dockers; nearly all the great writers of the day supported them; and funds came in from many sources. Eventually, the owners gave way on all the main issues, granting the dockers their 'tanner'. It was a turning-point in the history of trade unionism.

F Ben Tillett was one of the dockers' union leaders. He wrote about his plans in his autobiography, *Memories and Reflections*.

From day to day, I surveyed both sides of the river [Thames] and worked out a most colossal picketing system. I saw how the Thames could be made idle; how shipping could be held up and a thousand million pounds of financial power brought to a standstill. These were my dreams, my terrible dreams. Remember I belonged to an outcast class, exploited, starved, bullied, despised. It was necessary to plan social war.

1 a) What can you learn from source A about workers' clothing?
b) What kinds of work did these workers do?
c) Look carefully. What can you see in source A which did not exist in 1750?
d) Explain why these things could not have existed in 1750.

2 a) Which source gives evidence that membership benefited workers' families? Give a reason.
b) Which of the three pictures shows skilled workers? Explain how you decided.

3 a) Read sources E and F. Write down at least one opinion from each source. Explain how you know they are opinions.
b) Source E suggests various reasons why the strike succeeded. What are they?
c) What other reason does source F give?
d) What would you want to know about source F before relying on it? Give reasons.

15 POPULAR CULTURE

A London's East Enders dance to a barrel organ (1890).

In 1750, people living in different parts of Britain knew very little of each other. As far as Norfolk people were concerned, Cornwall might as well have been a foreign country. By 1900, people were reading the same newspapers and speaking much the same language. Britain had become a nation.

That was not the only change. In 1750, there had been roughly twice as many village labourers as town ones. By 1840, there were roughly twice as many town labourers as village ones.

In the countryside, people amused themselves much as they had done 300 years earlier. They danced round the maypole on May Day; there were competitions to find the best ploughman or the best runner. In the evenings, the menfolk went to the pub, as in this 1880 photograph.

B

In towns, too, the working class went out drinking. Pubs were open all day; children under 14 were allowed in until the 1890s. In some poor areas there was one beer shop for every twenty families.

Drunkenness was common. One wife went in search of her husband and found him drinking. Beside him stood their shivering daughter. He had pawned her dress to pay for the drink.

Apart from the pub, town streets were the main place of entertainment for the working class. There was plenty of music in the streets, too. Solo singers and bands added their sounds to the hustle and bustle of street life. So did the barrel organs, often accompanied by a monkey which collected the takings.

The railways made it possible to have days out at the seaside. Only the rich could do this in 1750. The richer working class might even have a week's holiday at the seaside in 1900. On the beach, crowds clustered round the Punch and Judy show, the stilt walkers and the performing animals.

But many Victorians did not want just to be entertained; they also wanted to learn. Magic lantern shows helped them to find out more about their country and its empire. These shows were the big popular entertainment of the late 19th century; the photographs here show you what people enjoyed watching.

C This slide is from a series telling the story of a woman married to a drunkard. Here, she thinks about killing herself. Lantern shows often warned about alcohol.

D Victorians loved performing animals. In this slide story, the dog on the right is on trial.

E A seaside scene in the late 19th century. Bathers changed in the huts, rather than in public.

F The most popular lantern sequence was 'the rat catcher'. The operator switched slides to make it look as if the man were eating the rats.

Except for source B, all the pictures are from 19th-century lantern slides. As primary sources, they provide an insight into popular culture in the late 19th century. Some show us Victorians enjoying themselves; all of them are evidence of what Victorians enjoyed. The historian must still ask how reliable they are.

1 a) What changes took place between 1750 and 1900?
b) What can you learn from these pictures about how life has changed *since* the 19th century?
c) What has stayed the same?

2 a) Choose one photograph which you think doesn't show a real event.
b) How does that affect its reliability as evidence?
c) Even so, it is useful to the historian. How? (You may think of more than one answer.)

3 a) What can we learn from these pictures about what Victorians enjoyed?
b) All the slides were made to entertain people. Which ones would *you* call 'entertainment'?
c) Why did Victorians find them *all* entertaining?

4 Think carefully and read the captions. What can you learn about Victorians' tastes and attitudes from (a) source C, (b) source D, (c) source E and (d) source F?

MUSIC-HALLS

Publicans soon realised that music could boost their profits. Actors and singers were hired to entertain the customers; music rooms were built specially for the purpose. Some publicans even built a separate theatre next to the pub – and the music-hall was born.

The music-hall appealed to the same people who went to the pubs. Even the most popular ones offered a cheap evening's entertainment. Balcony seats cost just 5p while a pint of beer was less than 1p. This painting shows one of them.

By 1900, they were the most popular entertainment for working-class people in the towns. Music was the main item on the programme. The most famous singers were treated like pop stars today. Many had started life poor, like Tilly Wood, who first danced in public when she was about five. Tilly was lucky: success came quickly. At 16, she was a star, earning up to £100 a week. She had a new name, too: Marie Lloyd.

Nowadays, we do not expect a singer to keep singing the same songs, year in and year out. We expect them to issue new records and change their act. It was different in the music-halls: people went to hear their favourite performers because they *did* sing the same old songs.

Also on the bill there were usually dancers or acrobats and speciality acts, such as jugglers or performing dogs, fire-eaters or mind-readers.

B The Farini acrobatic troupe are shown above.

The earliest music-halls were fairly rough places, often for men only; by about 1870, they had become less vulgar. They served food as well as drink and a 'star' name would attract people from miles around. The hall was lit by flickering gas jets: more than once, a hall burned down. The footlights burned lime: more than once, they burned a performer, too.

By 1900, many music-hall owners included moving pictures as a part of the show. Little did they know that moving pictures would be so successful that, in the 20th century, the music-halls would close down.

The halls may have gone but the songs remain. Their lyrics tell us much about working-class people of the time. After all, the singers were as working class as their audience. So the songs they sang were about things which the working class knew well. The sources on page 75 are from these songs.

C If you saw our backyard, 'What a pretty spot,' you'd cry.
It's a picture on a sunny summer's day,
With the turnip tops and cabbages wot people doesn't buy,
Well, I makes it on a Sunday look so gay.
Cos the neighbours think I grows 'em and you'd fancy you're in Kent
Or in Epsom if you gazed into the mews.
It's a wonder that the landlord doesn't want to raise the rent
Just because we got such nobby pretty views.
It really is a very pretty garden
And Chingford to the eastward could be seen
With a ladder and some glasses, you could see to 'ackney marshes
If it wasn't for the 'ouses in between.

D It's a great big shame and if she belonged to me
I'd let her know who's who.
Nagging at a feller what is six foot three
And her only four foot two.

He ain't been married not a month or more
When underneath her thumb goes he
Isn't it a pity that the likes of her
Should put upon the likes of him.

E Daisy, Daisy, give me your answer, do.
I'm half crazy, all for the love of you.
It won't be a stylish marriage – I can't afford a carriage
But you look sweet upon the seat
Of a bicycle made for two.

F Wiltons Music Hall was one of the first, built in 1856. This is how it looks today.

G A scene from a TV music-hall programme, recorded at a music hall.

1. a) Why were music-halls built?
   b) How did music-halls change during the 19th century?
   c) What change happened in the 20th century?
2. a) Look at sources F and G. Which one do you think gives us a better idea of what a Victorian music-hall was like? Give reasons.
   b) Is source A better than sources F and G? Again, give reasons.
3. a) Read sources C, D and E. What can you learn about working-class life from these sources?
   b) These songs were written to *entertain* people. Does that mean they are not reliable as sources? Explain your answer carefully.
4. a) What could a future historian learn about your generation from modern pop songs?
   b) How does our culture differ from the Victorians' culture? Give *at least* two differences and suggest reasons for these differences.

16 CHANGE ON THE ROADS

1750 1775 1800 1825 1850 1875 1900

The turnpike trusts had improved Britain's roads. But the railways had killed off the turnpike trusts. People stopped travelling long distance by road: they went by rail instead. By 1890, a few coach services were still running, but mainly to link with rail services.

Town roads were still well-used. In 1750, the rich travelled around town in a sedan chair or a horse-drawn carriage. The poor could not afford either: they walked. But, in 1829, there was a development which was to change city streets for good. The bus arrived.

The first ones appeared in London and were horse-driven. Fares were not cheap but better-paid workers could afford them. For the first time, workers could afford to live some distance from their workplace. Nearby villages soon disappeared as the towns spread outwards.

The first buses were quite small. They had just one deck and carried about a dozen people. By 1850, a second deck had been added, creating seats for ten more passengers. The picture above shows the inside of one. By 1880, the bus had the shape of a modern double-decker. Rows of seats went across it and passengers faced the front.

The bus brought freedom to the better-paid workers. The low-paid had to wait for the electric trams, which appeared in the 1890s. Then, they, too, could move further away – and the towns spread once again.

Meanwhile, in 1885, a young German engineer made an invention which would make road travel popular again in the 20th century. His name was Carl Benz and he built a motor car.

In 1886, he drove his car through the streets of Mannheim. The public was not impressed. When it broke down, bystanders advised Benz to stick to horses. The rich, too, laughed at him – and the police warned him to get off the roads.

It was 1894 before a Benz car first appeared on the roads of Britain. (It cost £80!) In 1896, the government put up the speed limit from 4 miles (6.5km) per hour to 12 miles (19km) per hour. Many people were not pleased. But the magazine, *The Autocar*, called it a 'red letter day'. It certainly marked the end of one era and the start of a new one.

B This photograph shows one of the earliest motor cars.

C Matlock Bath, Derbyshire, in 1890.

D Alexandra Stewart: *Daughters of the Glen* (1986). She was born in 1896 and recalls life at the turn of the century.

A lot of adults nowadays would consider our daily journey to and from school 'a long walk'. There wouldn't be many would walk eleven miles to and from Aberfeldy, all on the same day to hear Gladstone make a speech. Father did. There would be even fewer would walk 28 miles to Glen Almond one day and 28 miles home the next, leading a cow. Father did, at an age when some people have taken early retirement.

The emphasis on speed takes something out of life – and more if you replace animals with engines. [An] old ploughman said that he didn't know what loneliness was until he was put on a tractor, since before that he had always had the company of two wise horses. The faster you go, the more blurred is what you see.

From Woodend to Tulchan is a marvellous walk – all the better then when the roads were smooth and white and soft as velvet to bare feet in the cart tracks, free of the noise of engines, and no smells of petroleum or rubber to get up your nose.

One question which historians try to answer is whether a particular change has led to progress. The invention of the motor car is an example of technological progress: inventors could make something which they couldn't make before. That is a fact. However, whether it led to social progress is a matter of opinion.

E The same street in Matlock Bath, photographed in 1993.

1 a) Source C shows that *two* forms of transport were used then. What were they?
b) Now, look at source E. List the ways in which the scene has changed since 1890.
c) What has stayed the same?
d) What evidence does source E give of progress? Explain how you decided.

2 a) Look at source A. Are these people rich or poor? Give a reason.
b) List the ways in which this scene differs from the inside of a modern bus.
c) Look at your answer to (b). Which of these changes are evidence of progress?

3 a) Read source C. What do you think this woman felt about the arrival of motor cars?
b) Would she have felt the motor car brought progress? Explain your answer.
c) Why is it difficult to say whether a change brings progress or not?

4 'Inventions always bring progress.' Do you agree with this statement? Explain your answer in detail, with examples.

17 CHANGE AND CONTINUITY

1750 1775 1800 1825 1850 1875 1900

There were massive changes between 1750 and 1900. However, historians know that it is very difficult to generalise about the past – in other words, make general statements which are true of all places or all people. As you study the sources on these pages, look for change and continuity. Also, look for examples of changes not affecting everyone.

By 1850, 250,000 power looms were in use in factories and most handloom weavers had been put out of business. Yet, in Ayrshire's Irvine Valley, the story was different. In Newmilns, the number of hand weavers went up from 550 in 1842 to 952 in 1872.

This was partly because they had improved their machines to weave very complex designs. This photograph, from about 1885, shows William Allan at work.

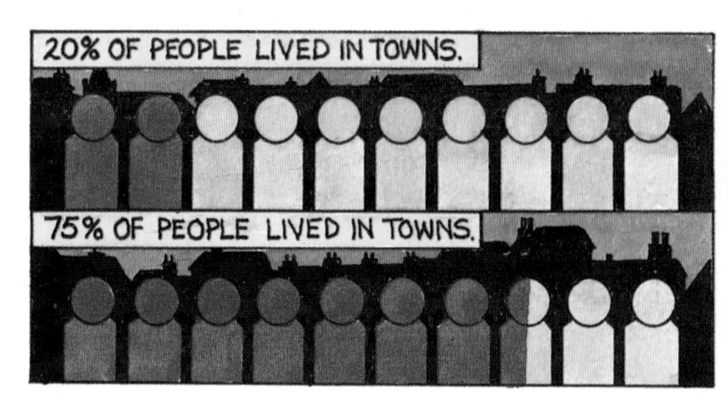

B Where people lived in 1750 (top) and 1900 (below).

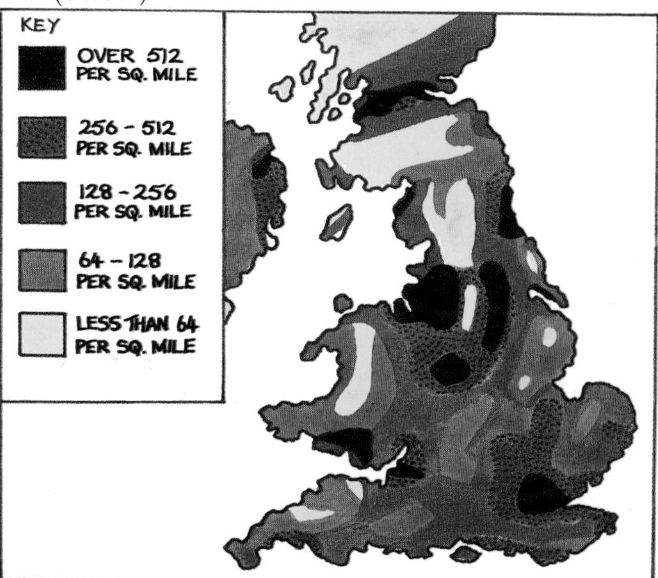

C How the population was distributed in 1900. In 1750, most people lived in southern and eastern England, where the land was most fertile.

D Ireland united with Britain in 1801. St Patrick's flag joined the Union Jack.

E How had the lives of factory workers changed? This is a typical day of a mill worker in 1900.

5.00 a.m. Woken up by the **knocker-up**. Get up and put the kettle on. Wash in cold water. Take the sleeping children to the child-minder up the street.
6.00 a.m. Factory whistle sounds and work starts.
8.00 a.m. Fifteen-minute break for breakfast.
12.30 a.m. Collect the children and go home for dinner.
1.15 p.m. Back at work.
4.30 p.m. Work ends. Do the shopping and cleaning, make tea and wash up. Do mending and prepare packed breakfasts. Put the children to bed.
10.00 p.m. Go to bed.

F About 250 million tons of coal were produced in 1900. This was more than 50 times what was produced in 1750 – yet 99 per cent of it was still cut by hand. This picture dates from 1892.

In 1750, most parts of Britain had a winter feast day but, for most people, Christmas Day itself was nothing special. All this began to change in the 1830s. The cracker was invented in 1840 and the first Christmas card (source G) was sent in 1843. By 1900, Christmas as we know it was practically complete.

But only for the well-off. Many poor people could not afford cards, trees or even presents. In fact, although Christmas Day was an official holiday, many people kept working. In parts of Scotland, the shops were open and the mills kept working. Children even went to school on Christmas Day.

Britain had been the first nation to have an industrial revolution – and production grew even faster between 1830 and 1900 than it had between 1750 and 1830. Britain was the richest and most powerful nation on earth.

But there were warning signs for those who cared to see them. Both Germany and the United States were spending more on state education than Britain was. Their national incomes were growing faster than Britain's. So they had more money to invest in industry. Britain's lead was disappearing fast.

There is one lasting reminder of those days when Britain led the world. In 1840, Britain launched the world's first postage stamps. As nobody else had them, there was no need to put the word BRITAIN on them. And, even today, British stamps are the only ones which do not have their country's name on them.

G The world's first Christmas card (1843).

1 a) Write down all the changes you can find on these two pages. Please write them on separate lines and in complete sentences.
b) Write out all those which you think would not apply to everyone living in Britain. Give reasons for your choices.
c) What does this teach you about the problem of writing about change?

2 a) Look at the changes you have listed. Which ones brought progress? Explain why you think they brought progress.
b) Were there any people who did not benefit from these changes? Explain how you decided.

GLOSSARY

abject – wretched
abolitionists – people who wanted to end the slave trade
ancestor – person from whom you are descended (e.g., your grandmother)
Anglican – of the Church of England
apprentice – person learning a craft or trade
atheist – person who believes that there is no God
baited – attacked by dogs
bankrupt – unable to pay debts
blast furnace – furnace in which iron ore is smelted
bondage – being held against their wishes
borough – town which has its own MP(s)
capital – money
capital crime – crime for which the criminal may be put to death
census – official count of the number of people in a country
cesspit – pit for putting sewage into
character – reference
charing – doing paid household work
civilised – more advanced in culture
colonies – countries ruled by another country
commissioner – official with a particular job to do
condensed – turned into water
corruption – bad conduct; dishonesty
corves – waggons or baskets
democratic – treating all classes of people as equal
depot – storehouse
dividend – share of the profits
domestic service – work as a servant in someone else's house
emigrate – go to live in a foreign country
empire – group of countries ruled by just one of them
enfranchised – given the vote
evict – expel (from their house and land)
excrement – human waste
exploited – used unfairly
export – something sold abroad
fallow – not growing crops
fictitious – made-up
franchise – right to vote
gauge – distance between the rails of a railway
Gothic – style of architecture using pointed arches and steep roofs
hectare – area of land equal to about 1.5 football pitches
humane – kind
immigrant – person coming to a country to live
impassable – not passable
import – something bought from abroad
inhabitant – person living in a place
inheriting – receiving from someone who had died
investor – person putting money into a company in the hope of profit
knocker-up – person paid to wake people up, by knocking on their bedroom windows
labour – workers
loom – machine for weaving cloth
magic lantern – machine for projecting slide pictures onto a screen
majorities – amounts by which the votes for one person are greater than those for someone else
mill – factory
nominated – chosen
nonconformist – any Protestant *not* in the Church of England
oath – solemn promise
over-hours – overtime
Parishes – districts, each with its own church
patent – document allowing only one person to benefit from an invention
patriot – person who loves their country
pauper – very poor person who cannot support him/herself
pawned – swapped for money, to be returned when the money was repaid
perjury – not telling the truth
petition – request
picketing – trying to persuade other workers not to work
pig iron – crude iron as it first comes from the blast furnace
plantation – large farm
poll – voting at an election
poop – deck above the ordinary deck of a ship
post-chaise – hired carriage
prize-fighting – fist-fighting before a paying audience
reconstruction – something made again
sempstress – woman who sewed for a living
sewage – human waste
shearing machine – machine for cutting the raised fibres off cloth
shoddy – cloth made of poor quality wool
speculator – person who invests in business
subdivision – splitting up into smaller parts
suckle – breast-feed
suffrage – vote
tanner – sixpence, now worth 2.5p
threshing – separating the grain from the corn
threshing machine – machine to separate grain from the corn
transported – carried
workhouse – building where able-bodied poor people had to live and work
wrought iron – tough form of iron with little carbon in it
yarn – spun thread